VOGUE

essentials

VOGUE
essentials

handbags

Carolyn Asome

conran
OCTOPUS

contents

introduction

the joy of arm candy

→ On the eve of World War II, the tricolour leitmotif of Horst P Horst's picture (August 1939) appears apt. Bags during the Thirties had become smoother and plainer, in keeping with the dominant American aesthetic of streamlining, which celebrated the new industrial materials such as plastics, Vitrolite glass and chrome. Coordinating accessories became a prevalent theme of how women dressed, with many fashion magazines featuring lessons on matching shoes to an outfit or to a bag. It was just as important for bags to be decorative as it was for them to be functional.

The legendary American *Vogue* editor Diana Vreeland once came up with the idea that women should dress more like men. The keystone of her thinking was "no more handbags". Women, she decided, would wear shirts with big pockets, jackets with big pockets, skirts with big pockets. It was all about putting the world in your pocket. She began rushing around preaching her new creed, but no one liked it. First of all, everyone panicked that leather manufacturers would suffer. Others pointed out that bulging pockets would hardly improve the silhouette of clothes. But what really persuaded Vreeland to back off was the argument that handbags are such a powerful fashion statement.

What's in a handbag? Quite a lot, actually. Not only are they eminently practical, but they are also the stuff of fantasy and dreams. Bags are at once the simplest and yet the most complicated of accessories – infinitely revealing of a woman's life. Former British Prime Minister Margaret Thatcher famously referred to her handbag as her "trusty companion", while it was a "handbag" that the architect Zaha Hadid cited as the one object she travelled with to make her hotel room "feel her own".

In recent decades handbags have become a powerful sartorial symbol, a social signifier of who we are and perhaps who we want to be, the subject of intense consumer desire, more revealing than our choice of shoes or even our winter coat (and, in recent years, certainly more expensive). Bags are also the style accent that rings the changes seasonally. As an icon of our post-modern globalized culture, handbags are venerated and ridiculed in equal measure.

AUTUMN FORECAST. FURS & HATS · AUGUST 9 1939 (16) · ONE SHILLING

VOGUE

↑ This *Vogue* cover by Eduardo Benito (February 1924) heralded the arrival of spring fabrics and original *Vogue* designs that celebrated an understated simplicity and smartness. By day the clutch bag, tucked neatly under one arm, flattered the body and kept the smooth lines of the new streamlined silhouette. By the end of the Twenties bags had become wider than they were deep. As a result of a new cosmopolitanism, bold designs from Africa, Egypt, Morocco and the Far East became popular in art and fashion.

← Few other fabrics hold as much allure as velvet, with its subtle sheen, promise of drama and subversive punk undertones. In this Rory Payne photograph (October 2013), the model wears a chiffon and lace dress by Vilshenko, a Diane von Furstenberg velvet jacket and Sonia Rykiel block-heel sandals. The capacious velvet and leather bag by Emporio Armani is typical of the size of bag required by today's women, who need to cart around all manner of tech gadgets, gym paraphernalia and flat shoes for the office commute.

"What are handbags for?" asked Vicki Woods in *Vogue* (February 2007). "For some women, a different bag is enough to change personality from day to day... obviously, handbags are mostly for the things women need to haul around with them – from money to makeup and Nurofen." She reported that the December 1949 issue of the magazine wrote excitedly about the new fashion for smaller handbags. It told readers that their new bag should contain "a pigskin cigarette case, a square mock-gold compact, pantomime tickets for *Miss Muppet* at the Casino Theatre, a gold-edged chiffon handkerchief, silver Dunhill cigarette lighter, tiny black and gold covered opera glasses by Asprey, a silver heart-shaped key ring, cigarette holder with gold trumpet".

Nearly 50 years on, *Vogue*'s then-editor Alexandra Shulman sent Woods an email (with reference to the piece): "My bag is vile inside, with crumbling cigarettes, chewing gum, receipts and pens that leak." Woods herself admits that if a man's hand goes near her handbag, even the man she's been married to for years, "I go into a kind of rape-alert mode and squawk. Women's handbags are public on the outside; utterly private within."

Bags first came into fashion in about 1800, when the full skirts of the ancien régime in France gave way to the slender, diaphanous dresses of the First Empire. Prior to that, bags had been uncommon since most women carried small necessities in the pockets hidden inside their full skirts – the pockets were attached to a waistband, and reached through slits in the sides of the skirt. It was only when the narrow, gauzy neoclassical style of dress eliminated the space for pockets that bags came into fashion. These early bags were known in England as "indispensables", because they contained crucial impedimenta such as fans and visiting cards and perhaps a small amount of money. No "nice" women wore cosmetics or worked in an office, so there was less to carry. As the 19th century progressed, the term "ridicule", meaning a type of small handbag, evolved into "reticule" and was used in both English and French until 1912.

By the mid-20th century, the average woman needed a larger bag because she was away from home more often, working, shopping and socializing. And, by the Thirties, most of the bags that we carry today had already been invented, including the classic handbag with its clasp frame and handles, the clutch, the satchel, even the shoulder bag. "Shoulder bags liberated the hands and were capacious enough for the practical needs of the working woman," writes Claire Wilcox in her book *Bags*, published in 1999

by the Victoria & Albert Museum. Elsa Schiaparelli was one of the first fashion designers to create a shoulder bag in the late Thirties.

For many designer labels, accessories, specifically bags, have become their biggest cash cow: many brands admit that at least 70 percent of their sales are down to bags. And while handbags might speak of conformity, they also speak of individuality. Take the affluent Middle Eastern consumer, for whom it is culturally acceptable, encouraged even, to show off their wealth via expensive clothes and accessories. But perhaps a bigger motivation is that for women wearing floor-skimming burkas, the only way to stand out is via sunglasses or bags with a jewel-like, decorative edge. Limited-edition accessories are important, which explains why one shopper, according to the buying director of a London department store, took all ten limited-edition bags, paying hundreds of thousands of pounds to ensure her exclusivity.

Bags have boosted the fashion business since the early Nineties like nothing else. Between 2000 and 2005, sales of women's outerwear rose by 12 percent, which sounds cheerful enough, but that is until you hear that handbag sales increased by a dizzying 146 percent.

According to Alicia Drake in *Vogue* (May 1999), the Nineties was the decade when accessories jumped out of the closet. One season they were fashion's unsung heroes, a harmless essential – let's face it, no one wanted to look greedy or too rich in the Nineties. The next they were reinvented as logo-bearing, waiting-list-inducing objects of global desire.

First up was Silvia Fendi, who introduced the Baguette and then its little sister, the Croissant, both fabulously decorative handbags, very expensive and quite hard to get your hands on outside Italy. Gucci revived the bamboo-handled Jackie O bag, and Milan became the centre of bag wars. In 1995 Diana, Princess of Wales, was given a Lady Dior bag, which caused a heady little It-bag rush for dainty pink-and-blue handbags (especially once they were renamed Princess bags). And when, in 1997, Marc Jacobs went to Louis Vuitton and turned the inaccessible super-luxury bag into a must-have fashion accessory, the whole world caught bag fever.

Phoebe Philo at Chloé began producing bags – first, the Bracelet, then the Silverado – made of worn-in leather and loaded with industrial-sized chunks of metal. She helped invent handbag hardware: the enormous great padlock that weighs half a kilo (1lb). Her bags hit the precise vibe of urban boho, a roughed-up

↑ This still-life painting by Giorgio de Chirico (January 1936), a modern artist of the time, details the likely impedimenta of a woman's clutch bag – possibly a debutante's. A Greco-Italian artist who lived in Paris, de Chirico was more famous for horses, broken columns and seascapes but here he illustrates a pair of Chanel's 16-button gloves and a pearl choker.

sweetness that was intrinsically very "London" during the early Noughties. For nearly £800 ($1,000), you could get a seriously cool street bag but at a luxury price. By the time Philo came up with the Paddington for Spring 2005, a whirlwind was waiting to happen. Newspapers reported that "must-have" was "can't-get"; every single one of the 8,000 Paddingtons produced for Spring 2005 was spoken for before even reaching the shops – in Europe, America and Japan. Averyl Oates, Harvey Nichols's bag buyer-in-chief at the time, told *Vogue* in 2007 that there were "something like 137 people waiting for a £794 bag". Net-a-Porter sold 376 Paddingtons online in the first 36 hours and had 700 names on a global waiting list. Their accessories director, Sojin Lee, remembers that "it was magic. Something about the Paddington elevated the Silverado and sales of that increased. We sell bags faster than clothes now." Sales of bags at Net-a-Porter hadn't merely doubled in the previous two years, they had risen by 400 percent.

Sometime in 2006, Tom Chapman, founder of the retailer MatchesFashion.com, moved the front door of his Notting Hill boutique. As Hadley Freeman reported in the *Guardian* (November 2006), after years of it opening into the clothing department, he decided it needed to be positioned a crucial couple of yards to the left in order to open into the shoes, bags and sunglasses. A minor adjustment, perhaps, but Chapman understood that there was "a real shift to accessories for customers and so I realized that it was important for the customer to be confronted with a lovely big wall of shoes and bags as soon as they come in, like sweets in a jar". In just two years, his total profits from those "sweets" had doubled.

Sales aside, Fendi's Baguette achieved cult status, provoking in-store tussles and appearing in just about every episode of *Sex and the City* and on every well-buffed shoulder, from Madonna's to Gwyneth Paltrow's. While instantly recognizable (the shape, the clasp, the abbreviated strap), the Baguette was also endlessly different. Coming as it did after seasons of homogenous fashion and Prada's black nylon, it revelled in extravagance, over-embellishment and individuality. "It's like a drug," said Italian actor Sophia Loren, proud owner of at least ten.

While the concept of It-bags weighing as much as 10kg (22lb), with their blingy hardware and four-figure price tags, may seem abhorrent today during a less bullish economic climate, bags still remain popular. Why do we love them so much? As she told *The Times* in 2012, clinical psychologist Anita Abrams has a curious

↑ The rise and rise of the micro bag, captured by Patrick Demarchelier (January 2014), shows the model Edie Campbell holding a miniature leather satchel by Prada. This new raft of micro bags encouraged women to leave the house carrying substantially less clutter and is a reflection of how society and the way we now live have changed: we travel lighter, carry cards, not cash and, for better or worse, spend a lot of time on our phones. The hands-free factor is another reason that has prompted grown women to embrace a satchel that one might usually associate – size-wise, at least – with a ten-year-old.

→ The opulence and candy-coloured cuteness of Fendi's Baguette bags signalled the death knell for minimalism and restraint and the advent of the millennium's It-bag era. Aside from spawning enormous waiting lists, the bags achieved cult status. In 2000, LVMH and Prada formed an unholy alliance and paid $900 million (£690 million) for a controlling share of the Rome-based luxury fashion house. Photograph by Paul Zak (March 2001).

theory that harks back to mankind's hunting and gathering stereotypes: "After many years observing the most successful presents I have given, I am baffled to note that boys and men tend to like anything that is vaguely phallic – umbrellas, pens or plastic swords – while girls love things that are womb-like, such as bags, baskets, things they can put things in."

We may no longer live in the It-bag era, but it's foolish to think we don't care about our handbags. For the foreseeable future, women will have to carry around phones and makeup, and want to do so with style. Proof positive of their importance (should that ever have been doubted) was Crown Court judge Zoe Smith's lament in 2012 that men don't understand their significance and that handbag theft should not be trivialized. Furthermore, in June 2015, a Hermès Birkin sold at a Christie's auction in Hong Kong for a record £146,716 ($222,912 at the time of sale), leading commentators to suggest that purchasing a luxury bag might be a safer investment than gold.

In 2008, just as the financial crisis struck, a curious thing happened to the designer bag industry. Handbags became more and more expensive, the wide gulf between an It-bag and a chain-store wannabe widening inexorably with seemingly nothing in between. Bag inflation (more than 20 percent a year on identical styles) careered ever northward. Suddenly, for the "I'm worth it" generation, £1,000 ($1,300) became the benchmark or "entry point" for a designer bag. It wasn't to last long. A backlash ensued and consumers saw the advent of the "mid-priced bag", which was the next bag phenomenon. Women still felt they were very much "worth it", but times were certainly changing – even the Russian socialite and fashion plate Elena Perminova was heard saying that she didn't own a Hermès Birkin because they were too expensive.

Initially, the mid-price bag trend was spearheaded by Michael Kors, the American designer whose Selma and Sophie MICHAEL bags (classic, sleek styles) sold for between £260 ($340) and £300 ($390). These totes have since sold in their tens of millions, making Kors – who nearly went bust in the Nineties – a billionaire many times over. His designs were glamorous without being ostentatious, aspirational without being too challenging and as functional as they were fashionable. Kors found a way to democratize luxury without devaluing it. That supermodels and celebrities carried his bags didn't hurt either, perpetuating the idea that a £350 ($460) bag could still be considered a style must-have – an attitude that has continued to flourish in recent years.

coveted
classics

"An icon bag is a friend for life – the still eye in the centre of a constantly buffeting fashion storm," wrote Harriet Quick in *Vogue* in 2003. Icon bags might be counted on two hands: Hermès's Kelly and Birkin, Louis Vuitton's Alma and Speedy and Chanel's quilted 2.55 and Timeless are some of the most instantly recognizable bags in the world.

It's not hard to see the enduring appeal of classic bags, especially those from a handful of French heritage labels. They exude a quiet, understated chic that reeks of old-world money and charm, with their set of unspoken but powerful associations and four-year waiting lists.

These classic bags announce membership to a club or a tribe, or at least to one that shares the same credit card limit. It's why brands such as Hermès have always enjoyed a huge cachet. Recent headlines that its Birkins hold their value better than gold have only sent the label's stock soaring higher still. Aside from status, spending a lot on a bag also buys you quality, since these classic styles are usually handcrafted from luxurious materials.

The first classic bags were limited in shape, sleek, boxy and ladylike. Says Valerie Steele in *Bags: A Lexicon of Style* (Rizzoli, 1999): "... after the war ended, many women went back to the home, and roomy shoulder bags were replaced by somewhat smaller handbags. These more petite styles were also in keeping with the ladylike look that was increasingly emphasized in the fashion press." Much of the fashion advice about bags recalled themes that had been well established by the Thirties. "Always

← At the dawn of the supermodel era, Stephanie Seymour, the quintessential glamazon, is adorned in quilted, gilt-chain Chanel bags and others by Rayne, a label to which Queen Elizabeth II remains faithful. Taken from the fashion shoot "The Great White Way", photographed by Sante D'Orazio (July 1990), this image reveals a new, glamorous and fresh template following the popularity of black. The shoot is prescient of the minimal Nineties and its predilection for the freshness of white, which was to characterize and shape the decade that became known for minimalism.

the simplest and most classic handbags are the best, and the quality of the leather is very important," was the counsel of Christian Dior's *The Little Dictionary of Fashion* (Cassell, 1954).

In recent years, especially after backlash against It-bag culture, many have become scornful of bags that cost thousands of pounds and that carry more adornment than you might find in Donatella Versace's jewellery box. Hermès's understated and less well-known Plume design has inspired a rash of niche brands, while stylist and *Vogue* contributing fashion editor Bay Garnett has reservations about bags that scream, "Look at how on trend I am and how much money I have" (*Vogue*, 2007).

"I love designer bags," she goes on to explain, "particularly classic ones that look a bit beaten up. I just don't like the thing of a bag being held up in front of the person as a status symbol. I like it when a beautiful bag is part of someone's life."

Currently, the vogue is for wearing a classic bag with nonchalance so that it, and particularly the wearer, don't look too precious. "It's like Kate Moss haphazardly gripping an evening clutch, chains wrapped around like a messy boatman's knot rather than elegantly swinging from her shoulder," says Harriet Quick (*Vogue*, 2009). "Or perhaps Chloë Sevigny, with an oversized, silk LV envelope casually scrunched in one hand in the manner one would hold a McDonald's takeaway, rather than a bag with the price tag of a second-hand car. Or Camille Bidault-Waddington, who at the spring shows carried her vintage LV speedy sack unzipped and stuffed under her arm like a child's teddy bear."

Classic stealth-wealth styles such as Bottega Veneta's The Cabat or Céline's Trapeze and Prada's Galleria remain popular. These simple models also chime well with a stricter economic climate in that they cannily scream "business" in the office but can still be carted to the farmer's market at the weekend with a degree of anonymity. But what confers classic status? Fashion insiders agree that the three ingredients are: a combination of legitimacy in the fashion industry, great advertising and celebrity support.

It will be no surprise that the five or six styles dominating the lust list – bags that could be described as "rites of passage", bought to celebrate first pay cheques or "big-0" birthdays – more than hold their value. Fanny Moizant, co-founder of Vestiaire Collective, the designer fashion resale site, says that the most popular model in terms of volume sold, currently retaining 70 percent of its retail price when resold, is the Chanel Timeless. The quilted Chanel bag with its "recognizable-from-a-mile-off" braided gold chain handle is arguably the status symbol of all time. It's testimony to Karl Lagerfeld's genius that he has managed to tweak both the Timeless and the 2.55 in recent years, endlessly reinventing them so that they are still the most coveted bags, worn by fashion's inner sanctum at the biannual merry-go-round of fashion shows and yet still very much desirable among CEOs and uber-coiffed Madame Chirac types, as well as affluent mums on the school run.

Coco Chanel designed her first quilted handbag with a gilt chain in 1955, and named it the 2.55 after the month and year of its introduction. It was made in Chanel's favourite colours of beige, navy, black and brown, and came in either leather or jersey. The chain handles, braided with leather, allowed the bag to be hung over the shoulder, leaving the hands free, in keeping with Chanel's overall design ethos that emphasized function and mobility. Such has been its enduring popularity that, during the Eighties, demand was so rife for the Double C's style that customers were limited to buying only three at a time in some stores.

Other major players are the Hermès Birkin and Kelly bags. The French company was founded in 1837 by Thierry Hermès, a harness and saddle maker, but by the 1880s it was based in premises on the fashionable rue du Faubourg Saint-Honoré in Paris. As cars replaced horses, Hermès began to produce other leather goods such as wallets and handbags. Now, it is a hugely successful, global brand. According to Moizant, the resale value of the Birkin bag peaked at 137 percent in 2015. How it came about is the stuff of bag folklore. The bag was introduced in 1984, after the chairman of Hermès, Jean-Louis Dumas, found himself on a flight with the actress Jane Birkin. She had just placed her straw basket in the overhead compartment but the contents fell to the floor, leaving her to scramble around. Birkin explained to Dumas that it had been difficult to find a leather weekend bag she liked and so they sketched an ideal prototype together.

The monogram and Damier check of Louis Vuitton, the French luggage and accessory firm, established in 1854, is also recognized the world over. The company's founder, Louis Vuitton, trained as a luggage packer for the best Parisian families – he was appointed by the Empress Eugénie – then went on to design and make luggage. LV city bags were derived from luggage, and some travel bags have became popular handbag styles, like the Noé. Originally created in 1932, the Noé was designed to carry five bottles of champagne.

↑ Just as the It-bag phenomenon explodes, Angela Lindvall carries a pale peach Chanel bag, which, for the next decade, will be a fashion-editor and front-row favourite, as beloved by fashion's inner sanctum as by socialites, grandes dames and affluent school-run mums. Appearing in Regan Cameron's "High Volume" fashion shoot (December 2004), this ultimate day-to-night bag is teamed with Chanel's peach pleats, a frothy concoction of silk chiffon and a graphic Chanel arm cuff. The outfit is typical of the femininity that was popular at the start of the Noughties, when a softer boho feel in fashion loomed large.

→ Mike Reinhardt (September 1978) captures an outfit typical of the Seventies disco era: a black silk crepe de Chine round-neck blouse and peg-top trousers by Hardy Amies, worn with a gold kid cummerbund and exuding a relaxed sophistication. Popular at the time were handbags such as this black suede envelope bag on a strap of black and diamanté from Charles Jourdan. Handbags that started out as handcrafted and idiosyncratic during the early Seventies were discarded in favour of those that were defiantly expensive and clearly identifiable as fashion became a serious pursuit for the professional woman.

← Neil Kirk (February 1989) captures the off-duty uniform of the late Eighties: the quilted Prada canvas bag made from black parachute nylon. Created by Miuccia Prada, who not only changed the bag-scape but transformed a once-boring, upper-middle-class Milanese label into a post-modern kingdom, this classically shaped bag is the perfect symbol of modern, industrial design combined with a passion for traditionally crafted products – ironically, these bag styles cost just as much as the

label's leather versions, if not more. It is shown here with a rubberized Agnès B cotton mac, a pair of Levi's 501s and a white cotton jersey M&S polo neck.

↑ During the bling-laden years of the mid-Noughties, the price of It-bags soared and they became the cash cow of many designer labels, for which sales of leather goods and small accessories typically made up 70 percent of turnover. A predilection for luxury skins became ever more popular as luxury goods houses attempted

to outdo each other in the quest to find rarer, more unusual materials. In some instances, skins were botoxed so that they were softer to the touch. Here, Thomas Schenk (October 2008) captures a "more-is-more" look: a Chanel snakeskin bag featured with Sass & Bide leggings, Jimmy Choo silver-studded boots, a cashmere sweater and a tulle body with a crystal-embroidered neck, both by Alexander McQueen. The vintage tiara is by Virginia.

↑ Mark Mattock (October 2004) snaps the suede Kelly Pochette handbag at Hermès, which was the new mini Kelly bag. The original Kelly bag was inspired by Grace Kelly, Princess of Monaco, and is perhaps one of the most iconic bags of the 20th century – a combination of demure simplicity and unabashed luxury. It was originally designed in the Thirties by Robert Dumas but, in 1956, Grace Kelly, recently married and scarcely out of the media,

appeared with yet another of her Hermès bags. Here was a golden marketing opportunity, so Hermès negotiated with the Monaco royal family to rename the bag in her honour. In subsequent decades, the Kelly has spawned a whole family of Kelly-style bags in some eight sizes, 20 different materials and a rainbow of colours and patterns.

→ Taken from the fashion shoot "Colour Code", photographed by Robert Erdmann (August 1989),

this image shows a quilted leather bag from Henry's teamed with an asymmetrically fastening orange wool coat by Yohji Yamamoto, and a cotton crew-neck body and metallic orange cotton and PVC jeans by Junior Gaultier. Red suede gloves by Dents add a theatrical touch, and chime with the "more-is-more" mantra to dressing prevalent at the time.

← ← Black is the new black: during the Eighties, there were few other alternatives to the slim black bag on a chain by Chanel or the Kelly bag by Hermès. What makes a great black bag? "It has to have body," said Coco Chanel of the classic 2.55 she created in 1955. "Sobriety should not be mistaken for lack of spirit," says Jo Ellison in *Vogue* (2008). "I love how it adds polish to my uniform of baggy jeans, a stripy T-shirt and flats, and makes my look deliberate and pulled together." In the same issue of *Vogue*, designer Anya Hindmarch describes a black bag as the "oil in the wardrobe", while Emma Hill, the then creative director of Mulberry adds, "Black is the jewel in the crown of handbags because of its immediate ability to transform a look from city to country, from day to night, or from inconspicuous to sexy." Photograph by Neil Kirk (October 1986).

↑ Monochrome mania hits fashion at the dawn of the Nineties. Here, Thierry Le Gouès (February 1990) photographs model-turned-actress Monica Bellucci carrying a Henry leather bag and wearing a black chiffon ra-ra skirt with a gold chain, a Chanel-inspired jacket from the chain store River Island, teamed with shoes from Johnny Moke. This classic, much-copied look filtered right down the style chain. Who didn't succumb to the swish of a chiffon mini skirt during the late Eighties or early Nineties?

Big, elaborate hairstyles and load-it-on gilt were very much the mood of the day.

→ Helena Christensen is placed in the spotlight by Albert Watson (January 1995) for the fashion shoot "Tux Deductible". Glamour is reduced to the bare minimum, the precursor to the androgynous style of fashion that exploded in the Nineties. Wearing a narrow, satin Ben de Lisi dress, cinched at the waist, a wool YSL Rive Gauche jacket and a simple black evening bag by Anya Hindmarch, Christensen epitomizes a new understated template for evening attire that obviated the need to load on the frills, ruffles, yards of taffeta and blingy excess.

← A fashion editor's classic, the Ebury was one of the first bags designed by Anya Hindmarch and named after a London street, as many of her original designs were. The bespoke version was created to mark the tenth anniversary of her first store and was the first piece that could have a handwritten message embossed inside. Intended to be passed down through the generations, the Ebury has evolved to incorporate other "family" members, such as the Featherweight Ebury, a modern lightweight style with loose pockets, tassels, embossed graphics and leatherwork techniques. There are also the Ebury satchel, Men's Ebury and the Ebury shopper. Photograph by Paul Zak (November 2003).

↑ Cecil Beaton (March 1954) captures the strictness of this mid-Fifties springtime suit made from charcoal and white tweed in the fashion shoot "Looks Like Spring". A top-handle bag – a structured, hand-held bag – is the accessory of choice here, evoking a clean, streamlined silhouette that was consistent with the primness of mid-Fifties fashion. It was arguably the Hermès Kelly bag that began the craze for top-handle bags. Despite its celebrity status today, the birth of the bag was muted. It took the glamour of a Hollywood (and Monégasque) princess, Grace Kelly, to transform it into an international, trend-setting must-have. Top-handle bags remain just as popular today, recalling a gentler, more ladylike fashion.

↑ The photography shoot "Fashion Currency Home Minted" by Frances McLaughlin-Gill (September 1962), in London's Trafalgar Square, celebrates the rise of ready-to-wear clothes. Here an outfit of dress and jacket in butterscotch amber tweed is shown teamed with black crocodile pumps and a black crocodile bag, both by Charles Jourdan. Reptile skin had always been a status symbol but it had become unaffordable during World War II. By the end of the Fifties, reptile-skin bags were back in fashion and a cornerstone of a woman's wardrobe. They were considered an investment that would stand a woman in good stead for many years to come, and were expected to age gracefully.

→ Helmut Newton (October 1957) captures Balenciaga's suit of the season: nubbly, black and waisted, it comprises a short, double-breasted jacket dipping down at the back and a skirt with a high, wide-hipped fullness, emphasized by the stand-away pockets below the jacket line. The model carries a top-handle bag, its streamlined shape chiming with the clean silhouette of Balenciaga's suiting. By the late Fifties, handbags were larger and clutch bags exaggeratedly long as hemlines crept up. The December 1958 issue of *Vogue* noted that "the bigger the better" is the new philosophy for the handbag buyer.

← David Bailey's iconic picture of Jean Shrimpton, taken from the fashion shoot "The Moods of Britain" (June 1963), shows her wearing a West of England flannel suit and a structured, top-handle bag by Finnigans. By the late Fifties, companies and shops began to specialize in handbags. There was Jane Shilton, H Wald & Co, and Finnigans in London; Roger Model in Paris; and, in America, Mark Cross, famous for the box bag featured in Hitchcock's 1954 film *Rear Window* in which Grace Kelly puts her negligee and slippers. In the early Sixties handbags were still enormous and mainly carried over the arm, with short, firm, single or double handles. On the whole, they were triangular at the base, narrow in width, and longer than they were wide.

↑ A typical ensemble from the Sixties, although it should be noted how modern this photograph by Eugene Vernier (September 1960) appears. This is an ode to jersey, which, according to *Vogue*, is equally suited to casual city and smart country dressing. The coat and skirt in ink-blue-and-black checked jersey is made from a fine wool by Valancay of Paris. With its topstitch detailing and leather, which has acquired a rich, weathered patina, the bag by Susan of Regent Street also recalls the style of bags popular at the turn of the millennium, capacious enough to carry the paraphernalia of the 21st-century woman and structured enough to confer a gloss on any outfit.

↑ Neil Kirk (June 1995) captures Helena Christensen in the mid-Nineties with a boxy monochrome bag by Lulu Guinness, wearing Capri pants that exude Saint-Tropez style and Manolo Blahnik sandals. Guinness, the quirky British designer, has won a legion of fans with her irreverent take on fashion, with bags designed in the shape of a circus tent, spider's web, butterfly and fan. During the mid-Noughties, she made annual profits of $8 million (£6 million), selling 100,000 handbags in more than 500 stores worldwide – a long way from opening her first shop in London's Notting Hill in 1986.

→ Arthur Elgort (April 1988) captures Christy Turlington in a double-breasted Chanel suit-dress of candy pink and contrasting apple green wool tweed bouclé. The style became the defining "armour" of the late Eighties, as popular with women smashing the glass ceiling in the workplace as it was with ladies who lunched with big pockets and even bigger hairstyles. A matchy-matchy approach to dressing was very much at play here, too, which is why the classic Chanel tweed bag, designed by Karl Lagerfeld at Chanel, is designed in the same fabric as the outfit. Also very fashionable at the time was fussy statement costume jewellery, evident here in the oversized pearl and gilt ear clips.

← The ne plus ultra of luggage, as photographed by Coco Capitán (February 2017). Jet-set style has long been associated with Louis Vuitton's suite of hard-sided monogram trunks, and it is a style staple that is still very much coveted today. In 1959, Gaston Vuitton, the grandson of Louis, developed a petrochemical compound to coat cotton canvas, which resulted in a durable, strong but lightweight material that could withstand the trauma of travelling. Fabric treated in this way could could also be stamped with the Louis Vuitton logo, and was used for the LV Steamer and Keepall bags.

↑ Hans Hammarskiöld's picture (May 1956) from the fashion shoot "Good Travellers – by Land, Sea or Air" depicts the stylish sterotype of travel. A model wearing a wide-necked sheath dress topped by a matching jacket in creamy beige wool descends the steps of a plane with a travel bag in tan hide from Fior. By the Thirties, many more people travelled by car, train and ocean liner than ever before. Elsa Schiaparelli was one of the first designers to respond to the challenge of producing lightweight travel accessories. She created "an entire trousseau in a specially designed Constellation bag weighing less than 10lb (4.5kg), which included a reversible coat for day and night, six dresses and three hats", as she revealed in her autobiography, *Shocking Life* (Dent, 1954).

↑ A modern-day reimagining of Fifties chic from the fashion shoot and article "Brighton Rock", photographed by Alasdair McLellan (November 2010). Here, the model Lara Stone wears a Valentino organza strapless dress adorned with florals, and a vintage handbag that recalls the decade when women routinely carried structured handbags on a metal frame of lacquered brass or steel. With the invention of washable plastics at around this time, handbags in pastel and pale colours became increasingly affordable for a wider range of society.

→ The monochrome polka dot was a dominant force in late Eighties and early Nineties fashion. Here is a dose of poolside glamour from the fashion shoot "Playing Pool" – swim strategy for civilized sun babes. A polka-dot Christian Dior one-piece swimsuit with a ruffled scoop back is teamed with black patent mules with circular mirrors by Tokio Kumagaï and a white leather bag from Loewe. The white picture hat by Graham Smith at Kangol adds an element of vim and flair. Photograph by Hans Feurer (July 1989).

← Peter Rand photographs this snappy Sixties outfit – a Van Gogh yellow tweed suit with pronounced collar from Jaeger – as part of "The New Impressionists" (February 1963), a fashion story introducing *Vogue*'s spring colours for that year. The model teams her outfit with a red bowler by Otto Lucas and a capacious black carryall by Charles Jourdan. The designer's large, deep, honey-blond crocodile bag of 1961, with its single handle and gilt-finished strap fastening, was typical of formal daywear, while his smart and capacious black suede and patent shoppers brought style to casual wear.

↑ Load on the leather is the message from *Vogue* and David Bailey's pictures (August 1974) for the fashion shoot entitled "There's a Change in the Leather". A tan leather jacket, nipped in at the waist, is teamed with a flared, gored and double-stitched leather skirt. To finish? A *bois de rose* felt hat from Saint Laurent Rive Gauche and Louis Vuitton's carryall. The LV Steamer and Keepall bags established a new era for travel bags featuring designer logos.

↑ Lisa Armstrong examines
how the truly glamorous travel
anywhere in the world armed only
with hand luggage and a cashmere
shawl. Such packing requires
extreme discipline, not to mention
a carefully curated assortment
of multi-tasking clothes that will
stand up to any occasion. Here the
model wears the jet-set traveller's
inflight wardrobe of choice: relaxed
fit trousers and a cotton T-shirt
teamed with deck shoes, all in
white, which exudes understated
style and an aura of simplicity.
The carry-on bag par excellence
is the Hermès Birkin, shown here
in white leather and canvas.
**Photograph by Fabrizio Ferri
(July 1994).**

→ The power of flowers is a fashion
perennial, as in vogue this year
as they were in the mid-Nineties
when this fashion shoot was
photographed by Pamela Hanson
(April 1995) in the Blue Mountains,
Jamaica. Supermodel Yasmeen
Ghauri adds elegance to a pink
rose-print polyester dress by Agnès
B, accessorized with a turquoise
cotton handbag. The mid-Nineties
saw a predilection for bags with
softer silhouettes, a step away
from the structured, boxy shapes
of the Eighties and a move toward
a grunge aesthetic that had a
profound influence on the music
and fashion scene of the time.

← Power dressing still loomed large in the mid-Nineties, although softer colours, as in this powder-blue satin wool suit worn by Yasmeen Ghauri, were beginning to gain popularity. Designed by the late Princess Diana's favourite designer, Catherine Walker, the suit's silhouette shows strong shoulders, teamed with a knee-length skirt. According to the style diktat at the time, suits were intended to dramatize the hips, legs and waist, and celebrate a more womanly way of dressing. The outfit is accessorized with an Anya Hindmarch blue satin bag, structured yet not too boxy. Matching your bag to an outfit was still very much in vogue, which explains the choice of silver strappy sandals by Imagine. Photograph by Neil Kirk (March 1995).

↑ Frances McLaughlin-Gill heralds the news on the winter-coat front at the dawn of the decade in the feature "Chic and Pretty, How To Be Both" (September 1960). Wraparound coats were a strong story from the Paris collections. This reversible version from Alexon in grey and white checks, edged in grey wool and braiding, is complemented by patent pumps, a white pillbox hat by Chez Elle and a mock-patent bag by Susan of Knightsbridge. The structured doctor's-bag style would inspire a whole raft of It-bags by Prada, Givenchy and Saint Laurent some half a century later.

↑ Eugene Vernier photographs the season's new suiting, with a focus on the pleated skirt (February 1956). In keeping with Dior's New Look, skirts are wide, long and full, a world away from the masculine-style, pared-down economy of wartime fashions. Up to 20m (22 yd) of fabric could be used for the skirts or dresses alone. Handbags that were wide, elongated and bucket-shaped were the accessories du jour. By the mid-Fifties, there was a far greater choice of leather available: crocodile, suede, antelope and patent, even lizard-grained plastic for those on limited incomes. A good plastic was considered a better buy than a poor leather.

→ David Bailey photographs a model wearing an outfit typical of the Seventies: a black suede shirt jacket and gored skirt, with cuffs and collar in stitched black leather, like the belt by Jean Muir, a matching hat by Graham Smith and a Louis Vuitton shoulder bag (August 1974). The first designer shoulder bags were by Elsa Schiaperelli in the late Thirties, but their functional military look made them favourites in the war years. As the teenage market began to swell in the Sixties, the formal fashions of the previous decade were replaced by those that appealed to a youth-dominated market. The casual shoulder bag was soon seized upon to go with the swinging new fashions, particularly the trouser suit.

↑ With the veneer of *Vogue* for a fraction of the price, *Vogue* Patterns allowed many women to wear the latest creations from the Paris collections. In this photograph (March 1949), Serge Balkin shows a dress and a full-length coat lined to match in judiciously juxtaposed shades of terracotta and spice – one for the slim dress and the coat lining, another for the flared coat of lightweight wool. This late-Forties ensemble is accessorized with a structured box clutch bag.

→ Named after America's most stylish First Lady, Gucci's Jackie bag paid tribute to Mrs Kennedy's inimitable style, which made her a darling of the public and fashion designers alike. This understated style was designed to be worn on the shoulder but also to fit securely under the arm. One of Gucci's best-selling styles today, it was called the Constance bag until 1961. While at Gucci, Tom Ford relaunched the Jackie bag in 1999 after it had spent years in hibernation, and Frida Giannini debuted the new Jackie in 2009. Photograph by Raymond Meier (March 1999).

→ Christy Turlington combines uptown fabrics with downtown style in this Central Park fashion shoot photographed by Regan Cameron (November 1999). The capacious, scarlet patent leather Louis Vuitton tote adds to the wow factor of this outfit of asymmetrical leather jacket and boot-cut trousers by Richard Tyler. Giant shopping totes were a sign of bags to come, when working women would require something quite substantial to hold all their paraphernalia.

← Kate Moss has single-handedly transformed how we view leopard print – in fashion terms, at least – rendering it a fashion neutral and a wardrobe staple. Shown here with a Max Mara double-breasted coat and Manolo Blahnik patent Mary Jane stilettos, she manages to combine a Sixties retro look with a modern-day edge. The photograph was shot by Juergen Teller (August 1994) for the feature "Small Wonder", about how Moss turned fashion on its head. There are no prizes for guessing that the bag – possibly a vintage find – is Moss's own.

↑ Taken from the fashion shoot, "Morale Boosters" (August 1960), photographer Don Honeyman captures the key looks for Autumn/Winter 1960. The sartorial counsel given by *Vogue* to its readers is that a light wool dress in a pale fabric (shown here in a cream bouclé), teamed with a full-length leopardskin coat, is the look of the season. An oversized handbag in tan cowhide from Susan of Knightsbridge is the recommended finishing touch. Bags, on the whole, were larger in the Sixties as women began to enjoy busier social lives and a growing independence.

↑ Have you got the memo about sleeves? "They may be puffed up but we'll take the bags flat," says *Vogue* at the start of 2017. Coco Capitán's picture (February 2017) illustrates the current mood for utility-inspired fashion with clothes that tap into shades of oatmeal and tobacco contrasted with black – often referred to in fashion speak as "modern timeless classics". The cropped silk jacket and ruched maxi skirt are by the Australian designer Ellery, who is based in Paris, while the boots are by Loewe. Shown here is the

very modern way to cart around everyday paraphernalia: a small bag – this one is by Nina Ricci – and the "overspill backup" – a very chic shopping tote by Céline.

→ Cara Delevingne reinterprets the power of pink in the fashion shoot "Pink Lady", photographed by Walter Pfeiffer (September 2013). Playing up to a Noughties take on the Sixties, she is dressed head to toe in a playful pastiche of bubblegum pink and polka dots by Miu Miu, complete with Bardot bouffant hair, pink suede and gold

leather boots, and a Jacquard and leather bag. "Modern pink is complicated," says Jess Cartner-Morley in the *Guardian* (March 2017). "The Pinkstinks campaign takes a straightforwardly oppositional stance, targeting the role of pink-saturated marketing in railroading young girls into painfully narrow stereotypes. But a new generation of culturally aware young women are taking a different approach to the same problem, subverting or reclaiming pink."

← In true Park Avenue style, opt for head-to-toe coordination in the wispiest of fabrics. From the fashion shoot "Street Smarts", photographed in Central Park by Carter Smith (March 2003), timelessly elegant shapes, sweetly chic colours and luxurious materials denote an uptown chic. Tuleh's polka-dot silk georgette dress and matching belted overcoat with Charmeuse lining are perfect. Finish off with white coral, pink sapphire and diamond Christian Dior earrings and a most ladylike tweed bag from Chanel.

↑ Channelling the elegance of Truman Capote's "Swans", this weighty white piqué dress by Susan Small, with graduated ribbing, cap sleeves and a flared skirt, is an outfit that, according to *Vogue*, would "take in most summer occasions with classic calm". The black cartwheel hat by Simone Mirman complements the clutch bag, epitomizing popular styles of the time. The importance of accessorizing and colour coordinating was high on the style agenda. Matching ensembles to accessories was very fashionable, and companies such as Rayne provided shoes and bags in any colour. Photograph by John Sadovy (April 1954).

adorned &
bejewelled

← During the Fifties, Europe
was desperate to show Hollywood
that it knew all about glamour.
Women were enthralled by the
apparently perfect lives of
the silver-screen goddesses
such as Veronica Lake, Joan
Crawford and, later, Grace Kelly,
Marilyn Monroe and Ingrid
Bergman. In this photograph
by Henry Clarke (January 1956),
Dior's mastery of haute couture
is evident: brilliance on brilliance.
A white satin stole, heavily
embellished with myriad
gleaming pearls, is worn with
a clutch bag made out of the same
"Cinderella-shall-go-to-the-ball"
fairy-tale fabric.

"Flash back to Milan, March 1997," observed Alicia Drake
in *Vogue* in 2001, "to the Fendi Autumn/Winter show, when
down the catwalk came a cluster of glittering handbags swinging
saucily from the models' shoulders. Covered in scarlet sequins,
embellished with embroidery and bearing a showy, coolly abstract
double 'F' clasp, there was a sexy insolence to these bags' flaunt-it-
stance. As observers sat contemplating the shock of sheer opulence,
you could almost hear the tolling of the death knell of restraint."

"It was the start of a new movement," creative director Silvia
Venturini Fendi told British *Vogue* in 2001. "It signalled the end
of minimalism and the start of a new era." On the catwalk, bags
started to get equal billing with the clothes and, more often than
not, became the season's defining item. As the *New Yorker* pointed
out, "Since the turn of the millennium, the role of the handbag
has changed from that of useful but peripheral accessory to the
absolute object of desire."

A couple of years later, in 2003, one anonymous fashion
journalist at London Fashion Week wrote, "Everybody, everybody
is talking about handbags with the intensity of cardinals
appointing a new Pope." If each fashion generation has its defining
silhouette – the elongated lily shapes of French designer Paul
Poiret in the early 1900s; the shoulder-padded Forties and
Eighties; the full-skirted New Look of the Fifties – then the
silhouette of the first years of the 21st century was sleek and long
and linear, with volume added not by a bustle or a big hat but by an
enormous, bulging bag.

"Some Baguettes are insane," said Vivienne Jones, Harrods' fashion accessories buyer at the time. She identified it then as the shop's best-selling bag ever. "Some are so heavily embellished, but they are always the ones that go first. It's all about having the most outrageous" (*Vogue*, 2001). Silvia Venturini Fendi had a different take. "The more they cost the more they sell," she told *Vogue* in 1999, a theory confirmed by a Browns sales assistant, who told of a crocodile Baguette with a price tag of £5,000 ($6,500) that survived just three hours in the store before being snapped up. "It's huggable, snuggable," said one Baguette fiend. It's more than a possession – it's your pet."

Of course, embellished bags are nothing new. They were popular in the Fifties, acting as a reaction against the austerity and shoulder bags of the war years. Although as Vanda Foster reports in her book *Bags and Purses* (Batsford, 1982), "In 1952, a woman who complained that tiny evening bags would not hold cosmetics and a cigarette case was told that 'any woman smart enough to carry this tiny handbag is sure of an escort who will provide the cigarettes'."

For many, bags were not unlike jewels. "The handbag can play the role of jewellery in completing an outfit," once declared Christian Lacroix, whose own bags were characterized by a couture-quality attention to detail. Precious bags, such as those by Jamin Puech, were made from tulle re-embroidered with sequins, or covered with hand-cut Austrian crystals, as were those by Daniel Swarovski. Moreover, just as different kinds of jewellery conveyed very different messages – grandmother's pearls versus a coiled metal "tribal" necklace – so, too, did different bags.

The classic evening bag of the Fifties was made from black satin or black velvet, often enlivened with rhinestones. The very rich could buy such bags with 18-carat gold frames set with diamonds. Indeed, in the past, wealthy women often carried bags made of precious materials – gold, silver, ivory, leopardskin – and all the great jewellers have made evening bags decorated with precious or semi-precious stones. And yet the appeal of these bags is not dependent on famous names or the incorporation of expensive materials – it is their artistry or charm, intended to appeal to our magpie instincts. Today's fun equivalent might be Anya Hindmarch's metal crisp packet with its inverse snob appeal but which is no less precious or pricey.

The definitive characteristic of precious bags is their size: a very small bag implies that the woman is being taken care of, like the Queen, who famously never carries money. There is snob appeal in smallness, which suggests discipline because precious bags are the antithesis of the practical, everyday survival kit and are consciously high maintenance, akin to wearing limo shoes. *Vogue Italia* compares the bags of the designer Ikuko Akatsuka to bonsai trees. They are like little sculptures, visual and tactile, to be placed on a table and admired like an object.

Recently, bags have become much more embellished, although in a non-precious, ladylike way, decorated with all sorts of furry trinkets, to inject a more fun, street approach. In 2004 Harriet Quick reported in *Vogue* that this new adornment included "photo badges, heirloom brooches, ribbons, fake flowers, chains and strings of pearls. The only rules were the more the merrier, as once-glitzy handbags were turned into walking geegaws. Against all the odds, this trend has run and run, hanging onto its cool quotient, well past its sell by date. Designers quickly locked onto the trend, producing their own trinket-laden handbags, which, like Chloé's charm-bracelet-strung shoulder bag and Gap's badge-covered satchel, soon become best-sellers."

It's a trend that has resurfaced in recent years with Anya Hindmarch's graffiti-style stickers and furry Fendi key charms. The rise of miniature minaudieres (for our increasingly cashless society) has proliferated; their size means one also needs to be possessed of a steely discipline.

Possibly the biggest sea change in recent times, though, is that precious bags are no longer simply reserved for the evening. They also bring a fantastical and humorous element to daytime ensembles and load-on-the-bling, maximalist dressing-up mantras that are so modish. Raffia might have been summer 2017's hottest material but the sell-out styles were those covered in trinkets, charms and an assortment of myriad jingles and jangles.

← The Seventies safari girl is the muse for this fashion shoot entitled "The Right Stuff", photographed by Raymond Meier (January 2008). The model is adorned in bangles, headscarves, tortoiseshell chains and a linen Oscar de la Renta dress, evocative of an *Out of Africa* ensemble. Tanner Krolle's African beaded clutch makes a fitting accessory; the London-based label had been creating classic leather goods for more than 150 years, but it was only during the late Eighties that it decided to reposition itself as an international contemporary leather accessories brand.

↑ Modern-day embellishment, Miu Miu style. In the fashion shoot "Siren Call", photographed by Norbert Schoerner (July 2006), the maverick designer Miuccia Prada plays with glitter and rhinestones. The very notion of how something precious or luxurious should be worn is subverted as the model takes one uber-embellished accessory adorned with sparkle the size of knuckle-dusters and wears it with extreme nonchalance, while practically nude, to the beach. Shoulder bags remained popular in the early Noughties, especially the 2.55 by Chanel; the fashion house launched its limited-edition 2.55 in 2005, to celebrate the bag's 50-year anniversary. It became the must-have item of discerning fashion editors and style influencers attending the biannual prêt-à-porter collections in New York, London, Milan and Paris.

↑ The rise and rise of embellished mini bags is evident in Paul Bowden's photographs (December 2014). Marrying high-intensity sparkle and low-fi shape, Miu Miu's huggable drawstring pouches in embellished suede are billed as fashion's new squeeze as demand for mini bags begins to grow. These jewel-like accessories, dinky finishing touches for an evening, also gained popularity for daytime as style aficionados looked to satiate their magpie instincts 24/7. For many women these bags are almost a crossover point between accessory and jewellery, while adding a playfulness to an outfit.

→ Prescient of the white manifesto that was to embrace the Nineties, the model in the fashion shoot "White Heat" (May 1989) wears a white cotton jacket over a sheer organza camisole and matching trousers by the designer Arabella Pollen. Given that this was photographed by Eddy Kohli at the tail end of the Eighties, however, there are, naturally, lashings of gilt. Chanel's quilted gold leather bag is the style of choice, while gilt also features in Butler & Wilson's link belt as well as the earrings and matching cuff by Mercedes Robirosa.

← Typical anti-chic elements from the queen of the unpredictable, Miuccia Prada, who references Harajuku cool with pink and red shift-dress-and-coat ensembles of thick duchess satin. *Vogue*'s Brit pack of star models, which includes Sam Rollinson, wear outfits teamed with top-handle bags – a core offering of the Prada brand. These bags are decorated with naive floral appliqué, like Japanese flowers in bloom, that adds a touch of whimsy to a shape that is eminently practical and structured, as suitable for the workplace as it is for the weekend. Socks worn with geisha-inspired flatform shoes tap into Miuccia Prada's predilection for "fugly" shoes and complete a tableau of bold, graphic colours. Photograph by Angelo Pennetta (February 2013).

↑ The perennial power of flowers is illustrated in Ben Toms's photograph (April 2013), which shows Stephanie Hall wearing the quintessential summer dress in layers of organza – "as beautiful as the Royal Botanic Gardens in bloom", according to *Vogue*. The Erdem dress is teamed with Dior's exquisitely detailed mini Lady Cannage bag. The beaded bag with crocodile handles takes 120 hours to make, and its flowers are painstakingly crafted from 900 sequins and crystals. It is, without doubt, the best in show at 30, avenue Montaigne – the home of the Dior brand.

↑ "More is more" is still very much the style memo from Vivienne Westwood at the start of the Nineties. Showcasing spring trends from 1992, the "Denim Now" fashion shoot, photographed by Sante D'Orazio (February 1992), features heavily made-up supermodel Niki Taylor wearing Westwood's Rococo-style printed cotton drill jacket, plunging satin corset, cuffed cotton shorts and faux pearl drop choker. Completing this maximalist take on fashion, before monochromatic minimalism takes its hold on the style agenda a few years later, is a drawstring bag featuring a print by the French painter François Boucher.

→ A feast of bold prints and colourful graphic geometric patterns, from the fashion shoot "The Sheltering Sky" in Morocco, photographed by Patrick Demarchelier (May 2008). Model Jessica Stam peddles a Noughties interpretation of Fifties bohemia and artistry. Marrying floral prints that clash, she wears a Christian Lacroix dress with ruffled detailing, teamed with Miu Miu's patent leather belt. Blue socks and sandals add a natty, idiosyncratic note to the outfit, while the suede and leather Louis Vuitton bag, with its nod to Fifties handbag architecture, is both capacious, stylish and modern. This structured bag for the modern woman is able to transport all the ephemera of modern-day living.

← Cindy Crawford, the ultimate power glamazon model of the early Nineties, oozes sexuality while posing for Patrick Demarchelier (January 1990) in a monochromatic shoot in New York City. She wears little more than a black one-piece swimsuit, with a deep V-plunge front, by Donna Karan, typical of fashion's minimalist mantra of the time. Accessories are kept to the resolute minimum: aside from a black dog, Crawford wears flats and a hat. Only the embellished tote with gilt decorative detailing from L'Or Noir suggests that this photograph might have been taken at the end of an era known for its blingy excess.

↑ For designers looking to the past, the swinging Sixties is a decade that remains an infinite goldmine of inspiration. These bag shapes never go out of style, and in 2010 they were still being reinvented with a modern slant. Valentino's slick white patent leather handbag, with its crystal clasp opening and sturdy, structured frame, and Miu Miu's blooming chrome, wool and patent flowers are shining examples of a modish, Sixties beat and just as covetable – perhaps even more so – some half a century after the main event. Photograph by Raymond Meier (August 2010).

↑ History doesn't record the moment when womankind first rose up and decided that December was the ideal time to incorporate some bling into her wardrobe. These days, metallics are for life, not just for Christmas. Nothing adds more vim to an outfit than the shimmer of reassuringly crunchy-feeling lamé or the twinkle of chainmail. Blazing a gleaming trail through the day, Regan Cameron captures Gucci's Sixties-inspired mini dress with crystal beaded flowers, teamed with Marc Jacobs shiny leather and jewel sandals and Fendi's gold and silver shopper, which all hold the allure of a candy wrapper waiting to be unfurled (March 2007).

→ Traditional heirloom lace and pearls are given a modern reworking in Mario Testino's "Lady Luxe" shoot (March 2012), where artisanal Sicilian know-how at Dolce & Gabbana is fused with glossy PVC fabric in this matching coat-and-shift-dress ensemble, which is also encrusted with Swarovski crystal. The crocheted top-handle bag from the Italian design duo is the perfect example of an accessory that references a high/low culture mix: not so self-consciously grand that it can't be worn with a pair of jeans but dazzling enough to be worn in pure, classic, ladylike style at the grandest of palazzi.

↑ Christian Dior's zebra-print bag, photographed by Raymond Meier in August 1999, is perhaps a portent of the ramped-up style of the early Noughties, when handbags ditched their minimalist design to embrace all manner of jingle-jangle trinkets and unusual animal skins, as luxury goods houses vied to outdo each other during the years of "It-bag" mania. Much like metallics, leopard print and many other animal prints had a neutral role in fashion, to harden or soften an outfit. The monochromatic effect of this bag, made from ponyskin, is particularly striking against the bold orange shift dress.

→ Alasdair McLellan (April 2011) photographs a model carrying a patent leather bag by Mulberry, one of Britain's success stories from the early Noughties. The driving seat at Mulberry is currently taken by Johnny Coca. He joined the British fashion and accessories brand in 2015 from the esteemed fashion house Céline in Paris and has introduced the Clifton, a natty chain purse, and the Chester, a ladylike top-handle bag. Prior to his arrival, it was Emma Hill who created a brand with a legacy that included the all-dancing Alexa bag (named after It-girl-about-town Alexa Chung), exuberant catwalk shows complete with celebrity front rows, advertising campaigns shot by Tim Walker, and shiny, happy flagship stores oozing English wit and charm.

← Claudia Schiffer smoulders with sensuality in this Herb Ritts picture (October 1989), part of the Paris couture shoot, "A la recherche du temps Bardot: a Parisian dream of a blonde, a boudoir, a boy on a motorcycle and a couture wardrobe fit for a star". Schiffer dazzles in an outfit by the ever-exuberant Christian Lacroix: a black silk damask fitted jacket, embroidered with tiny beads and finished off with a large chartreuse silk faille bow and jet-bead tassels, worn over black lacy cycling shorts. The finishing touch? A pink satin shoulder bag adorned with gilt and faux gems on a gilt chain.

↑ The beaded, snakeskin-trimmed Fendi Baguette bag, photographed by Thomas Schenk (September 1999), heralded the advent of It-bag mania. Every girl needs a little sparkle in her life, and it was the Baguette that caused a retail phenomenon and a stampede to the stores. At the turn of the millennium, according to Alicia Drake in *Vogue*, Baguette bags were selling at the rate of 75,000 per season, at between £350 ($450) and £5,000 ($6,500) a pop. Sales aside, they also achieved cult status. In 2000, LVMH and Prada joined forces to pay a monumental $900 million (£690 million) to buy a controlling 51 percent share of the Rome-based luxury house.

↑ Mario Testino captures Jacquetta Wheeler modelling Autumn/Winter trends of subtle, glossy embellishment and high-octane glamour for daytime (August 1999). A zip-front cardigan and a beaded skirt, courtesy of Karl Lagerfeld at Fendi, and a Ralph Lauren sleeveless top make up the cashmere layers, while matte sequins add an elevated yet understated polish to the sell-out Baguette bag. Fendi's Baguette signalled the end of minimalism and the start of a new era. According to Alicia Drake in *Vogue* in 2001, "From then on, everyone started to use and treat them like pieces of clothing."

→ A stylish supermarket sweep: Bridget Hall channels Fifties Riviera chic – Capri pants and cropped cardigan – in this classic pose with more than a dose of kitsch and bold, bright pop-art colours. Taken from the fashion shoot "See You in Miami", photographed by Ellen von Unwerth (April 1995), Hall's white stilettos suggest a retro feel, as does Gucci's white leather bag, which is small and impractical enough to add a high-fashion veneer to an outfit and typical of the simple, minimalist bags so popular during the mid-Nineties.

← Yasmeen Ghauri stands out in Gucci's sunflower-print dress, which *Vogue* describes as "the one dress shape worth investigating in 1995, a round-neck, sleeveless shift that hugs the figure from neck to knee". Captured here by Pamela Hanson (April 1995), it is teamed with tan Manolo Blahnik sandals and a vintage box bag with beaded butterfly appliqué from Paul Smith. The insatiable appetite for anything vintage, but particularly bags, was to take a grip on the fashion world, spurred on by TV shows such as *Sex and the City*, in which coveted vintage accessories became the Holy Grail of style.

↑ "I have kissed at least the hand of every beautiful lady in Europe," the Florentine aristocrat and designer Emilio Pucci once declared. He may well have exaggerated the kissing bit, but he had certainly dressed them all. During the Fifties and the Sixties, the wardrobe staple of many a style maven consisted of the kaleidoscopic pattern and distinctive swirl of a Pucci-designed garment. Fast forward to the Nineties, and Pucci enjoyed a style revival, captured here by Eamonn J McCabe (July 1990), with different Pucci prints on a dress, scarf and an oblong clutch, juxtaposed to create a visual assault on the senses.

↑ Gianni Versace's "molto sexy" figure-hugging swimsuit was standard attire for the glamazon models of the early Nineties, who stormed onto the fashion-scape and were immortalized in George Michael's "Freedom" video (1990). This gilt and print silk handbag was typical of Versace's designs of unflinching sensuality, which included bondage and pop-culture kitsch, along with a profligate use of embellishment, pattern, colour and ornament.

Here was a designer for the age, who catered for a woman's life, from the boardroom to the bedroom and back again, in a body-conscious, often brazen style that tapped into the fashion diktats of the Eighties and Nineties. Photograph by Tyen (July 1991).

→ Christian Lacroix, the exuberant French designer, demonstrates the artistry of his Eighties heyday. Supermodel Christy Turlington, photographed by Arthur Elgort

(April 1988), wears Lacroix's saffron linen curved suit, comprising a cropped jacket dotted with green buttons and an empire bubble skirt. The grosgrain handbag with blue-green ceramic fish adds a touch of whimsy and wit, a few years before the seriousness and monochromatic nature of minimalism took hold. Lacroix was famous for a palette of colourful Mediterranean clothes, reflecting his native Provence – here, his kooky elegance is very much in evidence.

→ The "I Am a Camera" fashion shoot (February 2012), photographed by Raymond Meier, examines the statement-making accessories of the style blogger. Shown here is an assortment of Miuccia Prada's accessories, all of which exude the wow factor and, typically at the time of the shoot, might very well be worn all together in the same outfit. The ne plus ultra of statement luxury is Prada's crocodile-skin bag. Rare skins – a sure badge of wealth – have long been a coveted bag buy and their popularity in recent years has not waned, despite the activity of animal rights groups.

↑ Jacquetta Wheeler models a turn-of-the-milllennium wish list of accessories, photographed by Lee Jenkins (August 2001). Prada's classic leather saddlebag is the coveted item, a style staple that once again inspired waiting lists more than a decade later. Saddlebags were first used with horses, then with bicycles and motorcycles as well, and many of today's fashion styles are directly influenced by the retro versions of the past. Saddle-influenced bags began to take on a new sophistication in the Eighties. Dressing for success meant having a bag roomy enough to carry personal organizers, calculators and calendars.

↑ The "more-is-more" mantra has never looked more appealing than in 2012, when shaggy, *Fraggle Rock*-coloured furs inspired goat-hair or shearling bags, shoes and key chains. Often these are all worn together in an explosive layering of colours, fabrics and textures, appealing to selfie-obsessed teenagers as well as their mothers. Fendi enjoyed a style renaissance with its popular furry pompoms, and other labels to lead the way with quirky accessories were British designers Anya Hindmarch and Lulu Guinness, and the faux fur label Shrimp. Photograph by Thomas Lagrange (August 2012).

→ The endlessly reimagined "La Dolce Vita" is captured by Emma Summerton (January 2008). Curvaceous Lara Stone models a taster of spring-season fashion, which taps into a retro Fifties glamour with enormous pin-up appeal. Marc Jacobs's sunny yellow two-piece is the outfit for a springtime promenade, teamed with Yves Saint Laurent's impossibly high Tribute sandals and gilt-chain-handle bag, a compact, go-anywhere style at the height of It-bag mania. Chain-handle bags were hugely popular in 2008, with every designer brand offering its own interpretation of the classic Chanel 2.55, some more literally inspired than others.

← From the fashion shoot "Light and Fantastic", photographed by Javier Vallhonrat (February 2008) in the Maldives. An urban baby-doll organza jacket-and-skirt-combo from Asprey, a sock-it-to-you eyeful of fluoro-pink pants by Paul & Joe, Jimmy Choo platform sandals and a textured 3-D clutch bag by Armand Basi conjure up pure fashion fantasy and whimsy in this sugar-almond palette – one part sci-fi to two parts retro.

As Vicki Woods explains in her 2007 article "It's all about the bag": "the bag you carry speaks for you in semaphore. The message from an icon bag used to be simple: 'I am old money rich.' Now it's more nuanced: 'I may be rich, but I'm as fashion-savvy as you are.'"

↑ In 1990 the froufrou excess of the Eighties was still highly visible, as shown in this picture from the fashion shoot "Coup de Poudre", photographed by Michel Comte (August 1990). According to *Vogue*, a sweep of summer pastels throws light on the perfect autumn wardrobe. A peach cashmere coat by Jasper Conran is teamed with silk slingbacks and a fluffy, lemon marabou-feather bag by 31 Février, illustrating that more is still very much more and will continue to be so until the march of minimalism comes to take its hold on the bag landscape.

← From the fashion shoot "Sweet Dreams", photographed by Nick Knight (May 1995), these are the dressing-up clothes for gracing summer evenings. At the romantic edge of fashion, they are also the stuff of fairy tales, with their clouds of tulle, acres of net and garlands of silken flowers. The model wears an eau-de-nil skirt over a long, gauzy chiffon skirt, which is ethereal and elegant and gently swaddles the body, from the master of tailoring and draping, Antonio Berardi. It is teamed with silk gauze gloves, with flowers on the wrists, by Basia Zarzycka and a beaded pale handbag by Daniel Swarovski.

↑ Beaded bracelets and bags form part of the Dosa Masai collection – a collaboration between Christina Kim, the fashion designer of the LA-based label, Dosa, and the Masai. This image by photographer Simon Upton is taken from "Safari Luxe" (February 2002), a travel story written by Susie Forbes, after she visited the Japanese-inspired interiors of the then newly opened Shompole Lodge in Southern Kenya, which represented the fashionable new face of eco-tourism. This particular collection was put together with the help of the Masai women at the nearby village of Oloordikalani, which translates roughly as "people of the red cloak".

→ → Day-to-night dressing was the focus in Arthur Elgort's "Round the Clock" shoot (September 1997). With a few choice pieces – a fur-trimmed coat, a crocheted sweater and a velvet dress – it is possible to move easily from day to night, according to *Vogue*. Karen Elson combines an exquisite mix of suede coat, lingerie-inspired separates, shiny gold sandals and an antique-looking beaded bag by Butler & Wilson. In the years leading up to the millennium, a sense of nostalgia perhaps contributed to the popularity of vintage items and retro accessories – the prettier and more decorative, the better – which were de rigueur for every discerning fashion aficionado.

← In his heyday, Christian Lacroix ruled the Paris couture catwalks with his tales of fashion exuberance and outfits that tapped into pure fashion fantasy. Here, he captures a look that is lively, short and seductive. Photographed by Patrick Demarchelier (October 1987), Naomi Campbell is wearing a pale lemon silk satin puffball skirt and a ponyskin bustier, which is swathed in a milk-chocolate jersey shawl, buttoned across the waist.

A brown suede bag, with a pleated edge and a gnarled twig handle, adds a whimsical, decorative touch.

↑ On the eve of the Nineties supermodel era, Linda Evangelista models that load-it-on Baroque that was so typical of the late Eighties. Appearing in Arthur Elgort's "Gold Nights" shoot (December 1987), the "more is more" mantra is evident in the choice of rich silks, sumptuous velvets and brocade that is embellished with fur, feather and jewels. The small gilded straw hat with dotty veiling by Marina Killery adds a natty eccentricity to an ensemble that also includes the quintessential Eighties evening wear staple, a strapless black top. Encrusted earrings, typical of the bold costume jewellery that was favoured at the time and a rich jewel brocade clutch bag complete the outfit.

↑ Once again, the mood is high-octane glamour, which in 1991 still owed much of its inspiration to pure Eighties excess. In "Perfect Pink", shot by Ellen von Unwerth (March 1991), a model teams a pink silk belted jacket with a tassel box bag by 31 Février and a gilt and pearl cluster necklace and earrings by Dominique Aurientis. Frivolity – Marie Antoinette style – is very much the order of the day here,

several years before black nylon backpacks and minimal bag shapes came to dominate the style agenda.

→ Thomas Lagrange photographs the most coveted bags of the season for the fashion shoot "Club Classics" (August 2012). Retro styles still feel right, as does plundering granny's attic for heritage-fabric, tweed and exotic animal-skin bags – all the better

to contrast with crazily patterned tights. Whichever style tribe you subscribe to, here are the high-velocity night-time dress codes of now, according to *Vogue*. The snakeskin bag is by Bottega Veneta, the tweed by Dior, the needlepoint by Dolce & Gabbana and the alligator bag is by Tod's. It-bag mania might be on the wane but there is still a place for investment bags with five-figure price tags.

masters of minimalism

Minimalist design was the prevailing mood from the mid-Nineties – a backlash against the hedonism and excess of the Eighties. Logos were removed or made discreet, and conspicuous spending was out (though it's a moot point whether the minimalist style was just as expensive to achieve as the ostentatious fashion of a few years earlier). Waif-like models and grunge clothes ruled the catwalks and fashion editorials, while colourful, two-tone, go-anywhere Hervé Chapelier totes or Tanner Krolle's leather graphic shapes were the arm candy of choice.

But, really, it was Miuccia Prada (a former Communist, feminist and student of mime, with a PhD in political science) who utterly transformed the bag-scape, creating the most coveted and defining bag styles of the decade: a pricey minimalist backpack and tote in black parachute nylon. Fratelli Prada had been making luggage and handbags for the affluent Milanese since 1913 and the shop near the Duomo was decked out with mahogany and brass fittings that were made in England. When Miuccia Prada joined the company in 1978 as a designer and shareholder, she decided to turn tradition on its head and make the company reflect her own uncompromising and idiosyncratic style. For her, luxury was not to be found in ostentation – anyone could do that – but in an almost monastic simplicity.

"One of the first things that Miuccia did," reported Lisa Armstrong in *Vogue* in 1993, "was to introduce a little zip bag with fancy gilt handles. Classically shaped, but made – and here was the masterstroke – in nylon, it was the perfect symbol of her love of modern, industrial design and her passion for traditionally crafted

← Classic investment buys are introduced in the shoot "Cache and Carry", photographed by Paul Wetherell (August 2013). The model's minimal, almost sporty-feel outfit – sleeveless cashmere coat with belt by Victoria Beckham and Miu Miu's wool gabardine dress – chimes with Anya Hindmarch's understated taupe tote bag. The backlash against the It-bag phenomenon in the late Noughties saw the rise of classic bags without logos, gilt and load-it-all-on embellishment. Popular investment styles were top-handle bags, which could be carried to the office and worn with conservative suiting as well as with more casual attire at the weekend.

products." As a former employer wryly noted, where Miuccia was really shrewd "was in making a bag that cost almost nothing to manufacture seem as desirable, if not more so, than the leather versions".

A few decades later, a similar phenomenon occurred in the form of Mansur Gavriel totes. At first glance, there was nothing remarkable about the small tasselled bucket bags in natural tan leather or the capacious totes with very subtle stitching and not a hint of hardware or logo. They were plain and very simple – you'd never guess that they were fashion's hottest item – and the fact that the totes cost a (very democratic) £350 ($450) was also a bonus.

By 2012 Michael Kors had cornered the market for the mid-price bag, but the ubiquitous style aficionados, hungry for something a little rarer, turned to Mansur Gavriel for sleek, minimalist shapes and pops of coloured linings – and the fact that the bags weren't so readily available. The brand didn't believe in waiting lists, either.

This was a sentiment that Tomas Maier, creative director of Bottega Veneta, had also acknowledged more than a decade earlier, with the invention of his 2002 stealth-wealth hit, the *intrecciato* (braided) leather Cabat: no logo, no hardware, no adornment – heck, not even a closure. For a handbag to be desirable, it also had to be scarce – a fact that new contenders in the field had to learn fast. "Women want a bag that is special and unique, not one that is seen in every store and on every other woman," he told the *New Yorker* in 2011.

Canny marketing, perhaps, or facing up to manufacturing challenges as a fledgling brand? Whichever way you looked at it, the New York bag label founded in 2012 by Rachel Mansur and Floriana Gavriel was onto a winner. When news of its latest e-commerce delivery was posted on its Instagram account one mid-December afternoon – a delivery that included every style and colourway available that season – 95 percent of the stock sold out within an hour. In what was surely an unrivalled bit of marketing – intentional or otherwise – a frenzy of customers took to the Instagram post to express utter glee that they had finally got their hands on a Mansur Gavriel bag or to say that they had missed out on buying the style they were after. Similar to Maier's approach, the strenuous refusal to over-market the bag was itself a kind of marketing – the type that appeals to the customer who disdains the easy status recognition that comes from a conspicuous logo.

In an increasingly saturated accessories market, few brands elicit such passion, obsession or, indeed, frustration. Design-wise, these classic, structured shapes speak of a stealth wealth that echoes the sell-out Prada Galleria or Céline Trapeze bags, except for the fact that, according to Natalie Kingham, buying director at MatchesFashion.com, "the bags are even more simple. They are so beautifully simple that it's impossible that they couldn't be worn with everything. That simplicity is really what the main attraction is – that and the amazing quality of leather, the nostalgia they evoke and those pops of colour in the lining, which are a bit like hard-to-resist candy" (*The Times*, 2015).

By the end of the Noughties, It-bags were – to the fashion cognoscenti, at least – starting to look very démodé. Style mavens at the shows, including the editors of French and American *Vogue*, would often sit in the front row holding just a mobile phone. One reason for this was that the weight of most bags – 10kg (22lb) and counting for some brands' styles – ruined the line of your outfit.

Utility bags are often said to be inspired by the urban environment, although currently they adorn the fashion pages of high-end editorial and appeal to all age groups. When they burst onto the scene in the mid-Nineties, these vest and holster bags were designed to mould to your figure, a bit like armour might, and were often inspired by flak jackets and bulletproof vests. The Nineties also saw a new group of British accessory makers emerge, in the tradition of the artist-craftsman, such as Bill Amberg, a leather goods designer. These styles remain popular today.

As Claire Wilcox explains in her book *Bags* (V&A Publications, 1999), backpacks have continued to be popular. "Comfortable and practical, they typified the early Nineties modern, minimalist approach to fashion, with casual accessories and an egalitarian feel. Men, women, students, tourists and ultra-fashionable clubbers could all find something to suit. Smart handbags remained small and shapely, with twisted-gilt bracelet handles from Saint Laurent, quilted denim from Chanel and the Hermès signature Kelly bag, miniaturized and worn around the neck like a trophy."

Functional cross-body bags made out of high-tech utility fabrics by influential designers such as Helmut Lang were also a welcome change for modern women. They were only too happy to be rid of prim handles and to embrace the new millennium hands-free and with open arms.

↑ *Vogue*'s fashion director Lucinda Chambers demonstrates her inimitable way of juxtaposing colour in her shoot "By the Book", photographed by Patrick Demarchelier (January 2013). Here, the resort collections in 2013 are explored, and Chambers shows how to team full, pleated skirts with mac-style coats. Flame-haired model Karen Elson wears a belted wool coat and viscose sweater by Jonathan Saunders, with a pleated wool skirt by Marni

and white wedge trainers by Jil Sander. The white tote, inspired by a doctor's carryall, is by Céline, whose minimalist-style bags made the label the go-to luxury brand for most of the Noughties.

→ In the Sixties-inspired shoot "Street Life" by *Vogue*'s fashion director Kate Phelan, photographed by Regan Cameron (November 1995), smart city fabrics – tweed, wool and leather – are teamed with bags and accessories

that are neat and simple. In the winter of 1995, the coat to wear was cream. The one worn here is a wool double-breasted style by Sportmax, with pale blue and grey check, boot-cut trousers from Joseph and chunky metallic leather court shoes by Russell & Bromley. The white frame handbag is by Miu Miu; its sleek lines and structured shape are typical of the bag styles that were popular during the mid-Nineties.

← For its high-maintenance veneer, the white bag is, perhaps, the equivalent of the limo shoe. *Vogue*'s analysis of bag styles that would resonate in 2014 included this coveted, must-have frame handbag by the Italian fashion designer Alberta Ferretti. Photographed by Angelo Pennetta (February 2014), it makes a striking accessory to the model's leather dress. Fashion designers have often dabbled with space-age styles that tap into the Sixties but these bags manage the masterstroke of looking both modern and classic. Nineties minimalism, some 20 years later in 2014, is here again enjoying its turn in the limelight.

↑ Dressed head to toe in Céline is how many style influencers and fashion editors liked to leave the house in 2011. In this photograph by Daniel Jackson (September 2011), the model wears a pair of skinny trousers and a two-tone sweater, while clutching a bowling bag by Phoebe Philo, who has long been a master at defining the sartorial zeitgeist. Once again, this streamlined silhouette is an interpretation of the Swinging Sixties beat. Philo is not the only designer to have been influenced by the bowling bag; some 11 years earlier, another fashion genius, Miuccia Prada, had a huge hit with the Prada version.

↑ Not many brands can get away with charging four-figure sums for a plastic bag. Then again, not many brands are able to intuit what the public will want to buy and wear long before they know themselves. This Miuccia Prada bag is strictly for show-offs and also, perhaps, an ironic take on the plastic beach bag. Modesty is saved by the inclusion of a creamy opaque purse. During the mid-Nineties, fashion mavens clamoured for the brand that made backpacks hugely desirable, and Prada still has the Midas touch, consistently setting the style agenda each season during the ready-to-wear shows in Milan. Photograph by Raymond Meier (February 1995).

→ What do you do when you can't afford a five-figure price tag for a couture dress? Wear white, of course. Why? Because head-to-toe white or even a white-top-and-trousers combo suggests a devil-may-care attitude to dry-cleaning bills, a life populated with wall-to-wall gophers and, perhaps, even access to a limo driver. The top in this shoot, photographed by Ben Toms (April 2013), is by CH Carolina Herrera; the cropped trousers are by Stella McCartney. Fashion editors know that white accessories at fashion shows will stand out to the paparazzi among a sea of navy, grey and black – until, of course, it starts to snow. The pristine white bags are by Hermès, Longchamp and Church's.

← In 2013 Karl Lagerfeld made a convincing argument for Sixties-style bouffant micro suits and kitsch accessories such as these plexiglass clutches. It's what Lagerfeld does so well and why his clothes – and bags – appeal to twenty-something style bloggers as much as to Madame Chirac types with their vertiginous Elnett helmets. Underneath his "street" veneer, which always looks so youthful, is the well-trodden formula of Sixties-style dresses, with capped shoulders, usually concocted from a shimmering white or pastel palette. His wit and sense of humour know no bounds when it comes to accessories, and he is always one step ahead of the zeitgeist. Photograph by Angelo Pennetta (February 2013).

↑ At least a decade before the rise of athleisure wear, the actress Mischa Barton, photographed by Regan Cameron (November 2006), looks street smart in a cashmere hooded dress by Lutz & Patmos, teamed with a quilted classic Chanel bag in cream. The gilt-chain bag enjoyed an enormous renaissance around 2006, when it was the most covetable bag for fashion editors to carry around during the ready-to-wear shows and when every chain store thought to include one in their accessories offering. A year earlier, the classic 2.55 was relaunched to celebrate the fiftieth anniversary of the birth of this iconic bag.

↑ A showcase of autumn's ode to all the shades on the Starbucks colour palette, photographed by Arthur Elgort (November 1992), this outfit demonstrates the season's gently deconstructed tailoring. The model wears a chestnut-coloured alpaca coat over a chocolate polo-neck rib sweater, teamed with classic beige gabardine trousers that recall the elegance of a modern-day Katharine Hepburn. A black leather circular bag with an animal-print centre by Gucci tonally matches the outfit. Animal-print bags, long a staple of a woman's bag repertoire, continue to be as popular today.

→ *Vogue*'s fashion director Lucinda Chambers shows how black lace, net and satin can still look glamorous long after the party is over. Mario Testino captures the model's attitude of complete nonchalance (November 1995). Once again, the style of the Sixties – a popular theme in the Nineties – is referenced, with a duchess satin evening coat and a lace shift, lined in peach satin, both by Neil Cunningham, which exude an understated sophistication. The red leather clutch bag is from a selection at Cornucopia; its elongated shape is typical of Sixties style.

← Paul Wetherell (August 2013) snaps the popular investment-style bags of the season in the shoot "Cache and Carry". Shown with an Hermès crocodile skirt, worn over a Burberry rubber shift dress, is Marni's slouchy leather backpack. After a decade of the punishing combination of high heels and heavy bags, stylish women had had enough. They may not have turned to orthopaedic shoes just yet – that was the following year –

but back-friendly backpacks were once again fashionable. In 2013 sales of backpacks in the London department stores Harvey Nichols and Selfridges were up by 30 percent.

↑ Laurence Ellis's photograph (April 2016) confirms that utility-inspired fashion shows no sign of waning. An oversize canvas tote bag with rope handles by FRAME is paired with a tie-up-front tunic

dress by J.Crew. Capacious bags or a second "overspill" bag were popular in 2016, due in part to the enormous demand for micro bags. These might suggest a disciplined approach to leaving the house and the rise of a cashless society, but the reality is very different when you factor in all the other paraphernalia that the working woman has to keep with her.

↑ Producing a roomy tote bag with stealth-wealth overtones was high on the agenda for most accessory brands in 2013, and the British fashion label Mulberry, which opened its second factory, The Willows, in Somerset that year, didn't disappoint. Named after the new workshop, The Willow was a roomy tote with a built-in clutch, to cater for the style conundrum of 24/7 dressing. Not only did it win over a raft of celebrities, it was the perfect go-anywhere, anytime bag for busy business executives. This version in navy leather and ostrich skin tapped into the predilection for impeccably clean lines, punchy primary colours and no-nonsense shapes. Photograph by Karim Sadli (February 2013).

→ Sonia Rykiel's gargantuan canvas carryall can pack it all in. In a shoot photographed by Coco Capitán (February 2017), *Vogue* heralds the classic shapes for Spring/Summer 2017 – the perfect white shirt (this one by JW Anderson) and trousers by Italian heritage brand Salvatore Ferragamo – along with shades of timeless tobacco and oatmeal. This is a style that taps into a utilitarian aesthetic, imbued with an heirloom quality that feels right for the season and beyond. Capacious totes are still very much part of the style expert's outfit.

← Model Sam Rollinson shows how Chanel's new direction embraces the spirit, according to Karl Lagerfeld, of "down-to-earth space globalization", or, in fashion speak, "wearable classics with infinite appeal". Once again, Lagerfeld turns to a tried-and-tested formula of Sixties shapes that combine both moody *noir* separates with womanly charm. Rollinson's tweed dress, captured by Alasdair McLellan (August 2013), is teamed with a Palmer//Harding cotton shirt, leather knee-length boots by Céline and a polished calfskin top-handle bag by Dolce & Gabbana, the very model of efficiency and style, referencing the bag shapes of the Forties and Fifties.

↑ Clutch bags have enjoyed an enormous style renaissance in recent years, channelling the chic and poise of the Fifties and Sixties. Stella McCartney's marble-effect, faux-leather version, photographed by Paul Wetherell (August 2013), is teamed with a pair of sporty-looking tread-sole pumps and a gabardine dress from Lanvin. As Harriet Quick, *Vogue*'s fashion features director, explains in "No Holds Barred" in 2009, the modern way to carry your clutch is to "grab it, scrunch it or dangle it", in order to affect a nonchalant panache.

↑ Monochrome mania never goes out of style, as Sudhir Pithwa's picture (November 2015) of Phoebe Philo's ultimate minimalist-style bag attests. Utility-inspired, this white (aka high-maintenance) canvas bucket bag has black leather trims, which exude a modern graphic polish. The origins of the classic drawstring bucket bag go back to at least 1900, albeit in the form of a beaded drawstring satchel, or reticule. Even more fascinating is the myriad of iterations the style took over the years, whether as a cloud of luxurious mink by Koret or as the perfect summer day bag complete with a wicker base.

→ Martin Margiela, the quiet, understated yet genius creative director of the esteemed French heritage label Hermès, here illustrates the perennial appeal of a white shirt and khaki shorts, modelled by Kelsey Campbell and captured by Tom Munro (March 1999). This cross-body bag by Miu Miu is typical of bags at the turn of the millennium, when the pace of city life dictated the need for clothes and accessories that moved as fast as you did and, crucially, allowed you to be hands-free. It is ironic that only a few years later women would be impeded by high-heeled platforms and weighty bags adorned with all manner of load-it-on gilt and embellishment.

← The days of corporate suiting are over with this rethinking of workwear. Interesting textures in an "off-palette" of colours are particularly arresting as they mimic the silhouette of the traditional two-piece. Edie Campbell, photographed by Patrick Demarchelier (January 2014), wears a spongy neoprene bomber jacket, an interesting partner to the full, pleated, knee-length skirt with a yellow satin band and a pair of pool slides, the year's shoe of choice.

Céline's Trapeze bag proved a big hit with style aficionados when it was launched in 2010. Capacious, graphic-looking and yet practical enough for carrying around everyday paraphernalia, it is another clear winner from the designer Phoebe Philo.

↑ In this image by Patrick Demarchelier (February 2014), model Sam Rollinson embraces the new style agenda for 2014, which included fresh prints, subversive details and touch-me textures, to herald a welcome change of pace. Organza doesn't need to mean wispy and romantic: Fendi's geometric handling of the lightweight fabric in punchy neon pink is a case in point. The black and white monochromatic shoulder bag, which recalls the Mary Quant era with its sharp, graphic lines, adds a visual focus to the outfit. Cat-eye sunglasses, also by Fendi, add a sense of nostalgia, yet this assembly of contrasting fabrics, textures and snappy shades looks bang up to date.

↑ The colour-blocking trend looms large in 2012. In this shoot by Josh Olins (July 2012), *Vogue*'s fashion director Lucinda Chambers shows how to energize autumn's rich palette of bordeaux, navy and mocha in a thoroughly modern way, with a youthful sporty spin bestowed on classic separates. The tweed jacket, with grain de poudre sleeves, and leather bowling bag are by Givenchy, while the satin trousers are by Yves Saint Laurent.

As Harriet Quick writes in *Vogue*, "The new way of carrying a bag is not to carry it all, but to 'wear it' with the sort of nonchalant attitude that the French have always affected so well."

→ Hermès's graphic weekender is just perfect for a spring getaway and is equally polished for breezing around town. This most iconic of bag styles, shot here by Karim Sadli (February 2013), is teamed with a leather sweatshirt and white gold ear cuffs by Repossi. *Vogue* reports that "in the world of accessories, impeccable clean lines, punchy primary colours and no-nonsense shapes are what matter now." Jean-Louis Dumas, CEO of Hermès from 1978 to 2006, once described Hermès bags as "useful in their elegance and elegant in their utility". The average wait for a Birkin bag is 18 months; it remains the watchword of luxury retailing.

← Minimalism the first time around, as photographed by Norman Eales (March 1965). The model wears a-black-and-white-quarter cloche hat, white gloves and a black suede handbag with chain handles, which no doubt references the classic Chanel bag. A classic black suede handbag was the foundation of a stylish woman's wardrobe. "What we want to capture", says Jo Ellison

in *Vogue*, some half a century later, "is the breezy élan epitomized by Kate Moss toting one of many black bags around town." Black bags are forever bags, and you don't need four, just one.

↑ The article "Lady Killers", photographed by Peter Marin (March 1995), reveals that the violent woman in life and on screen has become both a male pin-up

and a post-feminist sex symbol. This pink, see-through, top-handle tote echoes the minimalist style mantra of the mid-Nineties. Although this was a bag concept originally intended for the beach, many designers sought to include a kitsch see-through version in their accessories collections.

↑ *Vogue*'s fashion director Lucinda Chambers shows how winter's razor lines and inky hues make way for a softer silhouette and a palette of electrifying shades in "Colour Guard", shot by Mario Testino (March 2006). A Givenchy poplin shirt, worn with a full purple skirt, and an oversized Marni bag have almost caricature appeal. The emerald green leather clutch with its black floral appliqué strap is a Noughties update of retro styles.

→ During the early Nineties, the square-necked power suit was still prevalent. Arthur Elgort photographs this mauve version teamed with shorts by Thierry Mugler and accessorized with Gucci's purple satin bag and silver slingbacks by Russell & Bromley (March 1991). Bag styles at the dawn of the Nineties, before the popularity of Prada's nylon backpacks or Fendi's Baguettes soared, were still small and compact and took much of their inspiration from Chanel's gilt-chain bag or ladylike, structured, top-handle totes. Gucci bags were popular, not only because of the label's recognizable logo, but also because Milan was enjoying its turn in the spotlight as the fashion capital of choice.

← Prada's various capacious tote bags have enjoyed decades of popularity. "What we tried to do", explained Miuccia Prada to Lisa Armstrong in *Vogue* back in 1993, "was to come up with a look that was beautiful, but in a very unshowy way. We wanted to make things that were totally different from what people had been wearing." It's a formula that has stood the test of time.

Prada has pioneered countless sell-out bag styles, from its black backpack made from parachute nylon to its bowling bag and, more recently, its Galleria top-handle tote. Photograph by Laurence Ellis (September 2013).

↑ As Vicki Woods pronounced in "It's All about the Bag", photographed by Mark Mattock (February 2007): "In this country we don't wear fur or diamond-encrusted watches, but if you're rich, you don't want to look poor. A status bag is an obvious indicator that you are part of that exclusive club. Go for a classic shape in smooth leather or a glamorous style with a gold chain. Or there is the Hermès Kelly bag."

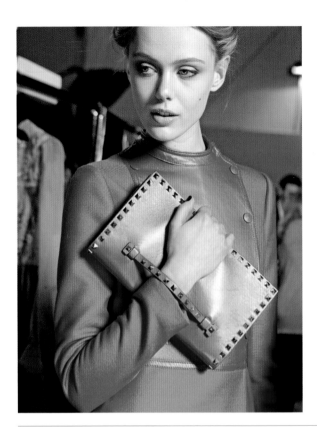

↑ Jason Lloyd-Evans photographs the season's most covetable bags (November 2012), and Valentino's studded oversize clutch comes out on top. Maria Grazia Chiuri and Pierpaolo Piccioli, at the helm of Valentino, managed to incorporate designer Valentino Garavani's aesthetics – beauty, glamour, elegance and perfect craftsmanship – and fuse them with the current style vernacular, which explains why a roster of celebrities and style influencers clamoured to the brand. With its smooth, sleek leather finish and glossy rivets, this clutch might look the height of sophisticated polish, except the way to "wear" a bag that year was anything but precious.

→ At the beginning of the Nineties, the Eighties shift power dress still ruled the corporate landscape. Liz Claiborne's orange rayon shift is teamed with Jimmy Choo leather sandals and a grosgrain top-handle handbag by Pelligrino at Place Vendôme in a fashion feature by Lisa Armstrong about the launch of Liz Claiborne, photographed by Neil Kirk (February 1991). In 1989 *Fortune* magazine voted Liz Claiborne Inc. the American company with the best return on equity. At the end of the Eighties, its merchandise was sold in 3,000 shops across America and Canada and turnover was around $1.4 billion (£1.1 billion).

→→ A procession of models with retro hair pleats and coordinating shift dresses from Jil Sander, Moschino and Giambattista Valli celebrate the power of red – the colour of the season in Emma Summerton's haunting picture (December 2009), shot at the foot of the weather-beaten White Cliffs of Dover. The main focus of the picture is the leather envelope stationery box bags by Smythson. Carried by all the models, they are symbolic of the fact that It-bag mania was at its height and a bag was very much at the heart of an outfit, on and off the catwalk, rather than simply being a mere accessory.

← *Vogue*'s fashion editor Tiina Laakkonen shows how animal prints add vim and verve to an outfit – especially in a splash of orange – in her "Animal Magic" shoot, photographed by Raymond Meier (August 1999). A giraffe-print coat by Philosophy di Alberta Ferretti has the wow factor, teamed with a pair of Jimmy Choo ponyskin boots and Gucci's ponyskin frame bag. The bag, which will add a pop of colour to more sombre clothing, has become one of fashion's jazzier neutrals, bestowing humour and visual interest to colour-block or understated outfits.

↑ How else do you bound into summer than with shots of acid colour? A belted leather jacket in fresh lime does much to pep up a plain black satin skirt, both by Christian Lacroix, teamed with a tangerine bag by Lulu Guinness. The British accessories designer is known for her quirky, idiosyncratic take on fashion. Her bag styles, according to Justine Picardie's interview in *Vogue*, include "a bag in the shape of a house, and then another, a turreted castle – they began to be seen on all the right arms, in all the right places: in the society pages of glossy magazines, carried by It-girls and young royals to the horse races at Ascot and premieres; flaunted by Demi Moore, Elizabeth Hurley, Madonna and Sophie Dahl." Photograph by Neil Kirk (March 1995).

↑ Some 15 years before micro bags enjoyed an enormous surge of popularity, J.P. Tod's (now Tod's) created a miniature ponyskin handbag. This accessories label is one of the most impressive recent examples of Italian fashion entrepreneurship. The company has mushroomed from a smallish family business into a global fashion juggernaut, so wealthy that in recent years it donated €30 million (£27 million, or $36 million) to renovate the Colosseum in Rome. Key to its success are its stealth-wealth-style bags, which include the D Bag, favoured by the late Princess Diana, and delicately soled, rubber-studded driving shoes. Photograph by Raymond Meier (August 1999).

→ Peekaboo cutouts ramp up the sex appeal of Rag & Bone's graphic, Nineties-inspired midi tube dress in the "Colour by Numbers" shoot by *Vogue*'s fashion director Lucinda Chambers. How else to build a splashy spring wardrobe? Prada has the answer with its suede and python shoes and striped leather bag. Miuccia Prada demonstrates that she has the rare ability to produce classic, sombre "investment" bag shapes, as well as possessing an unflinching way with colour and a love of graphic geometric patterns, creating some of the most irreverent, witty handbags on the fashion-scape. Photograph by Patrick Demarchelier (February 2016).

← Feast your eyes on a colour mashup! Patrick Demarchelier snaps breezy colour-blocking in all its technicolour glory (February 2016). A sheer, sky-blue, micro-pleated dress is layered over a sunny yellow turtleneck top, while resin bangles by Pebble London and Miu Miu's leather concertina bag add another colour jolt. After years of very minimalist fashion being top of the sartorial agenda, the maximalist revival, led by Gucci's Alessandro Michele, can be seen as the antidote to a year

dominated by political upheaval. *Vogue* rings the changes for a style memo that declares, "Choose any colour as long as it's bold."

↑ Paintbox brights were the building blocks of the wardrobe in 2014. Mulberry's envelope bag, as seen in this photograph by Angelo Pennetta (February 2014), is the firm foundation of any stylish ensemble. Envelope styles were once the preserve of corporate attire but not any more. This new breed of clutch bags is

surprisingly roomy, although a steely discipline is still required to ensure it doesn't end up looking too bulky. The clutch bag's supremacy in recent years has been fuelled by the fashion blogger, whose blogs depend on "street style" photographs, either of themselves or stylish others. Shoulder bags, handbags and totes can look notoriously untidy in photographs, even if the bags themselves are the height of elegance.

so

---

street

From the Sixties onward, the fashion landscape was no longer determined by the mighty couture houses. There was a disaffection with haute couture fashion, which seemed out of touch with the desires of most women or the reality of their lives. Many design cottage industries had started to emerge during this time, encouraged by the alternative lifestyles that were beginning to establish themselves, as well as by the feminist movement, which had become a force to be reckoned with. Naturally, fashion started to reflect these shifts in attitude.

Unisex, ethnic, New Romantic and casual looks all appeared during this decade, with handbag shapes a world away from the conformity and rigidity of previous eras. Music, too, played an increasingly influential role in the fashion of the young. In 1963 Mary Quant started her influential Ginger Group label, and her bags were made in black and white PVC and decorated with big dots or her signature daisy motifs.

Increasingly, there was a growing demand for craft in handbags, which was supported by the top designers of the day, such as Jean Muir, who included leather appliqué clutches in her offerings, while the Saint Laurent Rive Gauche collection featured monogrammed shoulder bags made of beige canvas and brown leather. Gucci, on the other hand, had leather-and-top-stitched shoulder bags with dog-leash straps. In November 1970 American *Vogue* reported that there was a demand for "combinations of fur and reversed calf; leather and webbings; a patchwork of lizard in scarlet, orange, Irish green and taupe".

← What other style capital peddles an eccentric boho fashion quite as successfully as London? Inspiration from the street and the city's many markets is at the core of this look. In "Paparazzo", photographed by Roxanne Lowit (December 2003), the world of Sophie Dahl is explored. *Vogue*'s contributing fashion editor, Bay Garnett, teams a Loewe cashmere sweater with suede trousers by Joseph, a Lurex hat by Just Cavalli and a crystal bag with fur lining by Escada. This bag may come with a four-figure price tag but the nonchalant way it is worn to the market is anything but precious.

Utility bags also became popular, inspired by a range of traditional, functional sources, including military equipment, tourist gear and sports accessories that had been modified for modern urban life. They were sculpted to hug the body as an extension of clothing. The first contemporary utility bag to become fashionable was the Prada backpack, as explained in the chapter Masters of Minimalism (see page 99). Unlike other design houses, Prada has always been more influenced by street fashion and youth trends. While the bag offered a pared-down minimalist aesthetic, it also quickly became an icon – its practical style and the fact that it was (and still is) made of Pocono nylon, an industrial-weight nylon, made it an unsurprisingly natural choice for a more "street" urban look. By incorporating young, hip and sporty elements into its design, it offered clientele of all ages a smart street style combined with the class, quality and exclusivity of a high-end fashion brand, catapulting the backpack straight into the fashion arena.

After backpacks became popular, designers adapted other street styles, including various kinds of waist packs and body pouches, which exuded a kind of pared-down, urban chic that was elegant, flat and also androgynous. It's worth noting, though, that while they were sleek when empty, these bags often looked lumpy when filled with anything more than a credit card.

In the past two decades, street-style bags have evolved considerably. This new era of the It-bag is decidedly modern, a combination of references that are at once casual and self-consciously anti-chic. We only have to think of the maverick Jeremy Scott at the helm of Moschino, who showed bags made from McDonald's French fry cartons and milkshake cups, Anya Hindmarch's Frosties cereal-packet bags, and the watering can, crab and cupcake clutches found at Kate Spade.

The work of numerous British designers, including Hindmarch and Lulu Guinness, reflects a typically British, quirky sense of humour. The Happy bags from accessories label Hill & Friends, created by Emma Hill, who for many years was at the creative helm of Mulberry during its It-bag heyday, come in leopard prints and bright, clashing colours with smiley-face locks which have eyes that twist and wink. Meanwhile, at Sophia Webster, there's a predilection for underwater-themed minaudieres.

Such bags are an integral part of an outfit for street-style bloggers at the shows, as crucial as the right brand of sneakers. As some of these designs testify, there is a still a strong appetite for novel, playful or even kitsch bags. Many consumers feel able to take more risks with bags than they dare with clothing, which makes them the perfect platform for embracing the potential of fashion for fun.

In 2016, designers such as Demna Gvasalia at Balenciaga incorporated the ubiquitous laundry bag into their high-end collections, offering a thought-provoking and ironic take on what the meaning of luxury is today.

The rise and popularity of cruise collections afford the bigger fashion houses the opportunity to create more fashion-forward designs. Chanel, for example, proposes both classic and novelty bags, the latter including the plexiglass Lego clutch of 2013 and the giant pearl bag of 2015.

While the death of the It-bag is always mooted but never quite materializes, one thing that is happening is that other accessories – shoes, boots and clothes – are now accorded more importance. In 2017, the anti-bag stance manifested itself in cloth tote bags – Anya Hindmarch's "I'm not a plastic bag" was one of the first cloth shoppers. The under-thirties acquire their totes from record labels along with their vinyl, while their mothers get theirs from organic farm shops or independent bookstores. They are increasingly thought of as the "overspill" bag, the receptacle in which to cart around your gym kit, the company laptop and a flat pair of shoes for the commute to work. Labels such as Marni – much in the vein of Demna Gvasalia – have also produced striped mesh shoppers, while the "second bag" market is also on the up as decorative, bijou handbags enjoy the limelight.

Whichever way you look at it, though, there will always be a demand for bags of some kind because the alternative – big, baggy, unsightly pockets, as Diana Vreeland, who was not often wrong, realized – is too ugly an idea in fashion to contemplate.

↑ If there is one fabric that dominated the winters of the mid-Noughties, it was shearling in every permutation. Here, Raymond Meier (August 2011) photographs the outfit of many a style hunter and fashion blogger in head-to-toe shearling to ward off a winter chill. That warm, fuzzy feeling has been reinterpreted by every luxury goods label: Céline's shearling tote was a sell-out, as were Tod's rolled-over sheepskin boots, which ensured you wouldn't be left in the cold. As for this sheepskin cape by Just Cavalli, similar styles were spied on every fashion editor, and shearling trickled all the way down the chain-store style chain.

→ In Josh Olins's fashion shoot (October 2014), directed by *Vogue*'s fashion director Lucinda Chambers, Marni's silver-coated, shearling coat possesses the wow factor, while street-style vibes are injected via the sporty Adidas sweatshirt, Marni trousers with the slouch factor and a shearling shoulder bag and tote by Chanel with graphic appliqué. Fuzz, colour, volume and texture are all part of this uber-luxe street outfit, which became the style uniform of the mid-Noughties, permutations of which have inspired twenty-somethings as well as mums on the school run.

← Zoë Ghertner's "Fresh Treasure" shoot (August 2015) explores the bag shapes dominating the style agenda. Punchy patchwork and bold alphabet and emoji appliqué adorn Louis Vuitton's Twist bag. Stealth wealth is out; covering your bag with jingle-jangle accoutrements, graffiti and stickers is in, even for grown women with serious jobs and a mortgage. Anya Hindmarch was one of the first designers to introduce stickers with a sense of humour – fried-egg shapes, smiley faces and various emojis – onto her classic bag styles, such as the top-handle Ebury. Style experts know to team these bold bags with sleek leather outfits and utility-inspired separates for a totally modern look.

↑ Tapping into the zeitgeist is something that Karl Lagerfeld manages with breezy panache each season. This multi-strand gilt-chain bag with its "street" connotations may be a world away from our perception of what the archetypal Chanel customer would wear, but Lagerfeld knows to mix up those tweed bouclé shifts with accessories that hint at a youthful modernity. Crucially, this most classic of bag styles needs to be constantly refreshed to ensure its "cool" currency. It also explains why this bag is teamed with cotton jersey jogging bottoms from T by Alexander Wang, as the rise of athleisure wear begins to take its grip on the fashion-scape. Photograph by Laurence Ellis (November 2013).

↑ Travel the world in style with the East West shopper by Louis Vuitton. Made from the sort of plastic-coated market bags used to carry laundry and household goods in Southeast Asia, this was a post-modern, thought-provoking take on luxury from Marc Jacobs in 2007, photographed by Mark Mattock (February 2007). What plastic bags lacked in environmental punch, they made up for in practicality and affordability. This was perhaps the precursor to versions by Demna Gvasalia in his debut collection for Balenciaga, about which, according to Vogue.co.uk, there were cries of foul play from the Thai fashion community, which pointed out that his oversized, striped bags were copies of the traditional market bag.

→ Printed trousers and a roomy Navajo tote will satisfy the frequent flyer's wanderlust. As fashion becomes more homogenized, style hunters seek out ever more individual and idiosyncratic bag styles. Top of the list are vacation finds sourced at the local market. Artisanal craft has also become a highly prized commodity, ensuring beautiful, unique bags with integrity, attention to detail and a suggestion of understated luxury. But, as many style addicts know, such bags are often three times the price of "look-at-me" designer versions with three-figure price tags. Photograph by Bella Howard (April 2012).

← Raymond Meier (August 2011) captures the enduring power of a fashion perennial, the polka dot. In 2011 dots were once again the print of the season, although they were no longer the twee pattern that would hover on the edge of the dance floor, getting up occasionally for the odd twirl as a homage to Fifties retro. Instead they were thrust to the forefront. The popularity of the collaboration between the then 83-year-old

Japanese artist Yayoi Kusama and Louis Vuitton (shown here in the blue-and-green polka dot leather bag) certainly influenced the fashion landscape. Here, a model wears a spotted Diane von Furstenberg jacket with a cotton shirt and wool trousers by Paul Smith. A bold red bowling bag by Burberry Prorsum adds a snappy jolt to this most graphic of patterns.

↑ In *Vogue*'s "More Dash Than Cash", high style is captured by Jacob Sutton (March 2010) at a fraction of the price. A striped dress from Acne is teamed with bead necklaces from Victor Caplin at Alfies Antique Market, London, and a cotton shoulder bag from ASOS, recalling the style of the global nomad.

↑ Fashion designer Christophe Lemaire's brilliantly subversive beaded shopper recalls a Seventies taxicab seat cover. Take it to the market with Marc Jacobs's acid stripe rugby shirt for a look that exudes pure street-style cool in a small American town. Having held a number of high-profile design roles within the industry, learning his craft at Christian Lacroix, Yves Saint Laurent and Thierry Mugler, with an artistic directorship at Hermès, Lemaire is now focusing on his own line: a wonderful combination of wit, understated style and "under-the-radar" clothes that have fashion editors clamouring for more. Photograph by Glen Luchford (April 2017).

→ "Red is cherries, the Coral Sea, my hair," the fashion designer Sonia Rykiel tells *Vogue*. It is also the colour of a girl's first lipstick, and red was back as the hottest makeup choice for winter in 2003. Nothing adds as much verve to an outfit or makes as definitive a statement. While red can look a touch too retro when combined with a rustling, Fifties-style *Mad Men* skirt, it works a treat with nude anything and slicked-back hair. This embossed Louis Vuitton leather bag in scarlet is a pure fashion classic. Photograph by Robin Derrick (December 2003).

← Who better to model autumn's sports-influenced fashion than Gisele Bündchen, wife of American footballer Tom Brady? In the cover story "She's Electric", shot by Mario Testino (December 2011), writer Christa D'Souza is pulled into the supermodel's force field. A few years ahead of the rise of athleisure wear, Bündchen illustrates the appeal of Thierry Mugler's cropped cotton jacket, a zip-up neoprene swimsuit by Lisa Marie Fernandez and a mini skirt by DVF. The pink and lime green chain-strap bag by Emilio Pucci has equal go-getting appeal.

↑ For some, patent leather with its subversive undertones brings to mind ageing rock stars and exotic dancers. But 50 years after the Swinging Sixties, the fashion allure of practical, "wipe-clean" patent leather is still going strong, as John Galliano's patent clutch bag for the House of Dior attests. While standard hides have had their place on the catwalk season after season, these high-shine iterations – from bustiers at Louis Vuitton to patent trench coats in every colour – feel literally shiny and new, and added a high-gloss veneer to fashion in 2003. Photograph by Robin Derrick (June 2003).

↑ In the fashion story "Secret of the Seychelles", photographer Norman Parkinson (December 1971) snaps a model in high crepe Manolo Blahnik heels and carrying a local basket. Any discerning fashion maven knows that true style doesn't need to come with a four-figure price tag, as this picture proves. Some of the most popular bag styles in recent summers are straw or raffia baskets, picked up for a song on vacation. Worn with a golden tan, they are go-anywhere bags that can be worn with anything. And you can never collect too many of them.

→ Everything but the kitchen sink! This picture by Mario Testino (January 2017) for the fashion shoot "Moonrise Kingdom" captures the globe-trotting model nomad with her mashup of an outfit. Photographed in the Mojave Desert, it manages to reference an elegant whimsy with pretty florals by Marni, a wool-silk sweater by Alexander McQueen, a pleated skirt by Sacai and a bohemian undercurrent. The bags on the model's back are idiosyncratic finds sourced from around the world.

index

acknowledgements

An Hachette UK Company
www.hachette.co.uk

First published in Great Britain in 2018 by
Conran Octopus Ltd,
a division of Octopus Publishing Group Ltd
Carmelite House, 50 Victoria Embankment
London EC4Y 0DZ
www.octopusbooks.co.uk
www.octopusbooksusa.com

Text copyright © The Condé Nast
Publications Ltd 2018

Design & layout copyright © Octopus
Publishing Group Ltd 2018

Distributed in the US by Hachette Book
Group: 1290 Avenue of the Americas, 4th and
5th Floors, New York, NY 10104

Distributed in Canada by Canadian Manda
Group: 664 Annette St., Toronto, Ontario,
Canada M6S 2C8

ISBN 978 1 84091 766 6

A CIP catalogue record for this book is
available from the British Library.

Printed and bound in China

10 9 8 7 6 5 4 3 2 1

Publisher: Alison Starling
Creative Director: Jonathan Christie
Junior Editor: Ella Parsons
Copy Editor: Helen Ridge
Senior Production Controller:
  Allison Gonsalves

Special thanks to Harriet Wilson, Brett Croft
and Carole Dumoulin at The Condé Nast
Publications Ltd.

Every effort has been made to reproduce the
colours in this book accurately; however,
the printing process can lead to some
discrepancies.

Unless otherwise stated, all text and
photographs are taken from British *Vogue*.

All photographs The Condé Nast
Publications Ltd except the following:

p2 © Mario Testino; p4 © Javier Vallhonrat;
p38 © Alasdair McLellan; p52 © Juergen
Teller; p66 © Angelo Pennetta; p73 © Mario
Testino; p75 © Alasdair McLellan; p77 ©
Herb Ritts; p78 © Mario Testino; p88 © Javier
Vallhonrat; p90 © Nick Knight; p104 © Angelo
Pennetta; p108 © Angelo Pennetta; p111 ©
Mario Testino; p116 © Alasdair McLellan;
p126 © Mario Testino; p130 © Jason Lloyd-
Evans; p139 © Angelo Pennetta; p145 © Josh
Olins; p152 © Glen Luchford; p154 © Mario
Testino; p156 © Norman Parkinson Ltd /
Courtesy Norman Parkinson Archive; p157
© Mario Testino.

Page 3: John Galliano's well-documented
ode to Forties tailoring is evident here in
the fashion shoot entitled "Pretty Woman",
with the sharp tailoring of a fit-and-flare
jacket and ultra-fitted, knee-length pencil
skirt captured by Mario Testino (February
1995). The fine check, faux leopard-print
hat, designed by Stephen Jones, and
the strictness of the black patent leather
handbag from Cornucopia are typical
examples of how the Forties were revisited
in the mid-Nineties, just as minimalism was
dawning and black, industrial-look nylon
totes and backpacks were about to explode
onto the bag landscape.

Page 5: Supermodel Shalom Harlow revels
in a prim, Fifties nostalgia, reminiscent of
a Talented Mr. Ripley filmset, wearing a
Rochas funnel knit in chartreuse, oversized
sunglasses, statement jewels and
a full skirt, adorned with demure florals.
Photographed by Javier Vallhonrat (June
2010), the leather frame handbag with
its clean lines evokes a bygone era yet is
strikingly modern, and its sleek silhouette
and structured shape comes as a welcome
relief after years of boho dressing. The
strictness and discipline required to carry
this chime with the prevalent mood in
fashion at the end of the Noughties, when
minimalism once again gripped the catwalk.

CAROLYN ASOME is a fashion and interiors
writer and brand consultant. A former
fashion editor at *The Times*, she now
contributes to the *Telegraph*, Saturday
Times, *The Sunday Times Style* magazine
and *Vogue*. She lives in London with her
husband and three children.